Praise for *Rebel Bookseller:*

Laties is witty, opinionated for sure, impassioned, but eminently practical in both his desires for independent bookselling and how to actually do it effectively. Activists of all stripes, not just booksellers, can learn from this book. It made me laugh. It made me think. It inspired me. —Ramsey Kanaan, co-founder, AK Press

Praise for *Son of Rebel Bookseller:*
Interlaced with the vivid imaginative writing Samuel Laties composed throughout his short life, *Son of Rebel Bookseller* is a testament to a father's love for his son and a chronicle of the search for meaning after devastating loss.—Lee Upton, author, *Tabitha, Get Up*

Praise for *The Music Thief:*
A lucid and wise coming-of-age memoir, in which the author searches for himself in the worlds of improvisational theater, free jazz, and Black liberation. But his explorations lead to a head-on collision with reality when he hears someone yelling, "Help, murder! Help! They're killing me!"—Seth Tobocman, author, *You Don't Have to Fuck People Over to Survive*

Praise for *Living Ur Sonata:*
Andy has made this extraordinary piece central to his repertoire, and this memoir recounts vividly his joURney with it, while offering a rich and insightful account of Schwitters' own.—H. Nichols B. Clark, Founding Director, Eric Carle Museum

WHICH WAY UP IS THIS?

FOR DANNY,
LOVE, ANDY

a bookseller's dream journal

ANDREW LATIES

Cataloging in Publication Data
Laties, Andrew
 Which way up is this? A bookseller's dream journal / Andrew Laties

ISBN 978-1-953465-06-1 (pbk.)
    1. Biography and autobiography—memoirs
    2. Body, mind and spirit—dreams
    3. Self-help—death, grief, bereavement
    4. Booksellers and bookselling—United States
    5. Laties, Andrew

Selected dream-journal entries, in original sequence, from September 2021 through January 2025.

Prefatory quotes:
William R. LaFleur. *The Karma of Words, Buddhism and the Literary Arts in Medieval Japan.* Berkeley: University of California Press, 1983. 4-5.

Front jacket illustration: "Which way up is this? Also, what is this?" by Samuel Laties

Cover design by Rebecca Migdal

First printing April 1, 2025
Published by Mythoprint Publishing
Easton, PA, USA, 18042

For Sarah

For Gaia

Buddhists of this period were interested in flattening or relativizing our habitual and easy distinction between what we identify as the *reality* of the world we experience when awake and the *illusion* of all the events that take place in our dreams.... Their claim and conviction was that the difference between ordinary waking consciousness and ordinary dream consciousness pales to insignificance when both of these are set in contrast to something else, namely, the consciousness of the mind that has achieved enlightenment.

—William R. LaFleur, *The Karma of Words, Buddhism and the Literary Arts in Medieval Japan*

FOREWORD

Still grieving eleven years after my son Sam's death, I agreed to try Jungian dream therapy. Never one to recall them, I strove half-awake to scribble dream-fragments into a notebook and narrate into my iPhone's recorder. Transcribing these, I sent them to my therapist.

The texts here are just as emailed—in their original time-sequence—though edited for grammar, punctuation, and name-change. I've left out the therapeutic conversations; your reflections are as valid as ours.

Did it help?

First: I was so grateful to experience Sam's presence in my dreams.

Then: yes, I did feel my unconscious perspective shifting, my conscious emotion lightening. The final dream seems to sum up this transformation.

Rebecca and I are being offered a theater space at a college—a lot of student artists and activist types will be working with us—and professors too. Mark D. is negotiating the rent with the person responsible for the price—this rent will be only $500 per month. I estimate the operation will have a $400,000 annual budget and I comment that we'll need to do a lot of fundraising—that there are many spinoff activities like media production—the possibilities are unlimited. Rebecca is enthusiastic and so are the student leaders.

I see a wall-display of quotes that the students have created, including one, "I want to burn in Hell," from the Buffalo bookseller Leslie P. I am curious about its meaning and learn or realize that it refers to an Oscar Wilde quote, "I want to burn in Hell with all my friends."

I say, "I want to burn in Hell with everyone I like, too."

Penthouse of large old hotel with complex interior
layout. I have an accordion hanging around my neck,
plus a clarinet portion that I'm blowing into.

I have climbed the back stairs and entered this
penthouse—and two older gay men are seated behind
a large round table that is covered with puppies. The
puppies are of various ages and colors. They all have
curly hair. They are sitting cuddled together. There
are several dozen crowded onto the tabletop. The
larger man is reading a picture-book to the puppies. I
begin to play the accordion/clarinet as an
accompaniment to this reading—just brief, quiet
accents and sounds, to emphasize the story. I do not
disturb the reading.

The puppies are falling asleep. When the book is
over, I apologize to the men for intruding, but they
didn't mind and are gracious.

I leave the penthouse and go down to the street
level. As I wander through town and enter other
houses, I am aware that Tibetan exiles—wearing long
brown gowns—they are Buddhist monks—have been
quietly entering many houses and silently engaging in
calming people down. I discuss with someone that
they are healing the town—they arrived from far away
and they began to simply do what they do—healing
the people and healing the world.

You asked to see my new iPhone. You were examining it, turning it this way and that, when it started smoking and burning. You held it as it bubbled and smoked and you started speaking to me—asking whether I was spending too much time on my phone anyway, why did I really need my phone, wasn't a phone a way to avoid the world, wouldn't it be best not to have a phone? Meanwhile the phone was burnt to a charred husk. I felt irritated but resigned—I knew you were right.

Then, you laughed and handed me back my phone in perfect condition. You said the thing that had burst into flame was a gag phone. They made these joke flaming phones in Korea.

Having given a successful speech as a white-haired
Rebel Bookseller old guy, I see a mirror and a mask:
a striped Mardi-gras (or Maori-ancestor) style eye-
mask, like tiger or leopard eye-mask. The mask is now
being worn on the face of a figure—we walk together
through a tunnel.

The shamanic mask-wearer is Death, but I feel not
fear, but rather surprise and some elation. We are
emerging from the tunnel toward brightness.

WHICH WAY UP IS THIS?

We have decided to take a trip. And I'm kind of not into it enough, but I'm kind of like going along with the idea that we'll take a trip, and I make the suggestion that we go to Paris, and we are—we've flown to Paris and we're in an apartment, and I'm very in-turned and Rebecca gets irritated with me for being so distant and in-turned and not even making a move to leave the apartment and go for a walk or something, because she had been going through guide books before we got on the plane and so she's familiar with a lot of different places that we might consider going, but she's not really sure where we should go. And so I say, finally, "Oh we could go anywhere, it doesn't really matter, we could just go to the Left Bank."

So then, we go out and we're walking, and I'm sort of not paying attention as we're walking through city streets, and it's—the weather is very, kind of, dark—it's the evening and it's cloudy, and maybe even rainy or damp.

And there's a lot of people around, and we're startled to see some people that we knew, someone like Katalina, who just happens to be there also, and they're all exclaiming, "Oh my gosh!" Or no, maybe it's somebody that I knew from the early eighties in Paris, who I've just seen, and it seems like they haven't changed at all.

And then, we're walking with a lot of people, there's a huge number of tourists there, we're walking along the river, and we've crossed a huge stone bridge, and Rebecca's feeling extremely engaged, looking kind of ravenously at places we're walking past, and I'm aware that she may not know exactly where she is—what landmark we're passing—and I say, "So, Rebecca, so you realize where we are?"

So, I'm lost, and I've snuck my phone out from my pocket to kind of glance at it, to try to see whether I can see on the map where we are. I don't want anybody to see that I'm checking a map function on my phone. And my phone does not display the map, and I feel like, "Oh, people are going to see that I'm looking at my phone; that I don't know where I am."

But then, I see from the picture on the phone that we're at the Pont Neuf, because the phone has shown me a simulation of rockets shooting back and forth from the different sides of the Seine, from a war that took place eight hundred years ago. Instead of showing me the map it's showing me a movie, or a sort of 3-D simulation.

So, I say to Rebecca, who's kind of walking along rather quickly—we're both walking among all these tourists, sort of, on this huge bridge structure: "Do you know where we are? Do you know where this is?" And just at that moment we can see a sort of fortress, looming up over the river, on the other side, on a sort of hill on the other side, and it looks exactly like a photograph that was in a guidebook that we'd looked at back home, and she says, "Is this the Pont Neuf?" And I say, "Yup, it's the Pont Neuf."

And we've reached the—sort of landing on a stairway on a sort of emplacement in the center of the river, and I'm trying to take a picture of Rebecca, and Katalina is there also, we've both decided to take a picture of Rebecca at the same time, who herself, is about to take a picture, so, as we take a picture, Rebecca is very irritated to have us taking pictures of her and she kind of twists her head away and starts to make a sound like, "Aaaaaa!"

And, as Katalina and I both press the buttons on our phones to take a picture, our phones make a sound as the shutter is going, like this, "Eeeeeee-eeeeee!"

And it's kind of dark, so the shutter, it takes a long time to take the picture, and Rebecca is making a face like she doesn't want to have her picture taken. And just at that moment—Rebecca and I are both on this landing on this stairway in the center of the Seine—Dad is there, sitting on a step.

And he looks like he's in his early forties, so he's got tight curly hair, and he's got a big smile on his face, and he's right there with us on the step, and

Rebecca sees him also, and I say, "Dad!" and then I look at her, and she says, "Dad!" and we look at each other and we're both a couple of inches from his face, and we realize that we both saw him at the same moment, and so he must be there.

And I don't know what to say to him; he's smiling, and we're there in the middle of Paris, and there's all these people around us, but we're just locked into this scene—seeing him sitting there, smiling.

And I say, "Dad, have you been here the whole time?"

And he looks at me, and he kind of shrugs, and then he says, "Well, it's like they say about Paris…" And then he has this quote and he says—and I don't know if it's an Oscar Wilde quote or a Maurice Chevalier quote—but he says something like this, he says, "It's like they say about Paris. To be in Paris is to be where there is—nothing like it in the whole world. And nothing really changes, and time is always true. When in Paris: then one sees the real joy in life."

I'm working in a house, and there's a fire burning in the trees, sort of a forest over behind the house. And there's a lot of work to do, and so I have a choice to make, and the choice is: "Choke, or Gamble?" That's the choice. And—it's kind of a paradox because it really means choke or burn. Because you would choke on the smoke, or you can burn up. So, the question is: should we run away from the house and stop working and get away from the fire, or should we just keep working and kind of tolerate the smoke, but get a little more work done. And that's the question: "Choke, or Gamble?" Meaning: are we just going to keep working up until the last second before the house actually catches on fire?

WHICH WAY UP IS THIS?

I'm living in the room in the hospital. Sam has died but his body is there with me, and we're on the bed together. And, I leave the room, and when I come back his body is gone, but just his arm is there. And I think, "Somebody came and took his body?" And I realize that I had seen a large bag, and that maybe someone had come and taken this bag, and that was his body. But how did they leave his arm?

Then, I'm sitting in the room and there's another guy there. And I have a different bag, sitting on a chair, and I say, "The bag is like this bag." And he says, "I don't see any bag there." And I pick the bag up—it's like the size of a garbage bag—and I press it between my two hands, and I say, "Like this, see, there's the bag here." And the man says, "There's no bag there. I don't see any bag." And I say, "But I'm pressing this—look how—see how far apart my hands are? The bag must be between, right?" He says, "No, there's no bag there." And I feel sorry that Sam's body is gone, and even his arm doesn't seem to be there anymore.

WHICH WAY UP IS THIS?

Okay I'm sitting at a table in a restaurant, talking to two guys, and they are—it's kind of like a business dinner, and these two men—one of them has dark hair, and the other has lighter hair—they're both about my height and we're all sort of having this friendly conversation among, sort of, professionals, so they're—each of them is sitting around, we're sitting around a table.

And I comment to the guy with the lighter hair that it's funny that he and the guy with the darker hair are wearing nearly identical shirts—they're dressed very similarly. And the guy with the lighter hair says, "Really? Are you sure?"

And then I look at the guy with the darker hair, and I say, "Yeah, look, he's got the—sort of a black shirt with—but with a herringbone white pattern—and you can see that he's got what looks like a tie—he's got a black tie with almost exactly the same pattern. And you've got—also—you've got this black shirt and this black tie, and you've got a little jacket though—but, so you're dressed almost exactly the same."

And then, the guy with the dark hair says, "Well, you're dressed this way too."

And I look down at myself and I realize that I also have a black shirt, with sort of a tie with this herringbone pattern.

And I say, "Well, we should be a—we should perform together. We should be a troupe."

And then I go: "Ba-dumm, dumm, dumm, dumm—" And then, I look at them, so that they can come in with sort of an a capella riff, so we can sort of start singing together, and I realize that the other diners at the restaurant are gonna be, sort of, surprised that our table suddenly erupts in a kind of a capella "Ba-dumm, dumm, dumm, dumm, bumm-DOH—Dumm-BUMP-bump." But, I don't care, because it just seems so obvious that we should be a troupe.

I'm at the front table of a large bookfair, which is taking place in a hotel ballroom or a large gymnasium—there are lots of tables, covered with books, and many shoppers—the bookfair has resulted in high sales.

People have been paying in cash, and I have a big white plastic bucket filled with loose bills—and also a big black plastic garbage bag, which has fresh green large-denomination bills bundled in stacks. This bag is more than half-filled with bundles of hundred dollar and twenty-dollar bills. A huge amount of money, in cash.

I have been keeping this bucket and this bag right behind my chair, where I'm sitting, at the front table—I have been handling all the transactions myself, and I'm very aware of the risk of having so much cash right there where it could be stolen.

But I must dart out from the table to straighten books on various tables around the room, which have become messy due to all the shopping. I'm anxious about leaving the front table, but I must.

I return quickly, only to see that my two employees, Jan G. and Jan D., have engaged with the bucket and the bag. Jan G. has added lots of loose paper garbage to the bucket of banknotes because she thought it was a trash can. I bark at Jan G. to stop—it's not trash. She backs away alarmed. I

19

take the bucket back, and as I rapidly paw through the bucket, I can see only crumpled papers, and no cash. I think, "Well, that was only the small bills. Loosely piled. It wasn't so much money."

I then turn my attention to Jan D. She has gathered the black trash-bag's top together and is beginning to carry it away, to throw it out. I shout and grab at the bag. Jan D. is unperturbed. She says, "Andy," in a chastising voice, yields the bag, and gives me a squinty-eyed, judging look.

I open the bag and see that there is a large machine inside that is actively shredding the bundles of banknotes into tiny slices. It looks like freely-working snowblower blades, hinged like jaws, chomping and chomping—systematically biting the bundles of money. The bundles of money are totally sliced up already, and the machine is actively slicing the pieces into even smaller pieces. Nothing can be salvaged.

I close the bag and hand it back to Jan D., who accepts it (glancing at me with a look of vindication) and leaves.

I collapse into my chair at the front table, feeling hopeless.

The bookfair is still going on actively around me. I realize that I am going to have to keep going on running it.

I'm in my bookstore and I realize that a large monkey is wandering through. It's—a spider monkey? Large, light-brown, lanky body—the size of a four-year-old child—with a very long tail. It is moving slowly and seems unconcerned.

A customer walks out the front door and the door stays slightly ajar. The monkey approaches the front door and pushes through it, outside onto the street. I rapidly move to the front door and pull it closed.

The monkey turns and notices me, inside, through the plate-glass front door. He looks at me and seems to wish to re-enter the store. But I don't want to let him back in—he is not my pet, anyway—and although he's been mild so far, I know that monkeys can wreak havoc.

WHICH WAY UP IS THIS?

I'm in a large hotel—maybe I have been running a
bookfair or attending a conference—I need to use the
elevator, and I go through a service door and see a
service elevator. I push the button and when it opens,
I enter. There are two people in there who evidently
work for the hotel.

As the elevator goes up, I become uneasy. The
elevator door opens on the roof, just as the two
people are revealed to be demons, who I realize
intend to eat me.

I am pinned on the floor of the elevator, with the
door now opened onto the roof, and I see that the
demon pinning me down is attempting to read a flyer,
on the ground. He is sounding out the words
incorrectly. I twist my head around and help him read
the words—the words have the letters H - G with
various vowels in between, and they spell words with
various odd slang meanings, which I interpret to him.

He says to the other demon, "This one could be
useful. He is clever. Maybe we shouldn't eat him."
Then he says to me, "Since you are so clever, can
you explain Mysterious Traces?"

I am delighted that I have a chance to escape
being eaten. I say, "Yes, when the universe—the solar
system—was formed, all the planets and sun were
spinning around, and the Mysterious Traces are all

the leftover from that—including the planets, and all the asteroids."

At this point, a girl can be seen to sing the names of the planets: Venus, Mars, Jupiter, Saturn, Pluto. I say, "Don't forget Mercury—and don't forget Armorica! Remember that Armorica is the planet out past Pluto."

I am flying through space with the demons, and I am pointing to the planet Armorica, which is all lit up with gigantic technological-looking buildings on its surface.

A group of us are in opposition to the government, and we are creating a secret newspaper. We cannot use conventional computerized printing systems because then we would be detected. Instead, we dig out old, broken printing press materials, from a closet, so as to print our newspaper by hand.

I now need to travel over a winding road through a mountain pass to get to a workshop/factory where an older craftsman works with his team making typefaces and inks and parts for hand-printing presses. I arrive, and I place an order for several complete sets of typeface/font.

I have traveled by sled, and I must leave right away, but I will return in one day, to pick up my order, when it is ready for pick-up. The printer-man is confident that he can get my rather large and unexpected order picked and packed in one day, no problem. His team will be working through the night on it. I then remember to order extra ink.

On my sled ride back across the mountain pass, I have brought certain printing-press parts with me, on my sled, and I stop for a break at a sort of garage. The printing-press parts keep slipping off the sled. I want to tie them on better with bungee cords, but I need to borrow these from the people at the garage, and I especially do not wish them to learn of the underlying purpose of my travels, which is opposition to the government.

I do get the printing-press parts tied down better onto my sled, however, and now I return to the workshop of the typeface-maker. There, I see the type he has packaged. It's a beautiful, curved package, and I recognize the Regina font, and the Awakening Glyph at the center. It's a sort of Sanskrit glyph/letter.

Rebecca's phone-alarm is going off... I understand that the Awakening Glyph I am seeing is associated with waking up.

I am blowing my Tibetan Monk's Horn, for a child who is with Maya Angelou. I want to blow it like the Tibetan monks do. I extend it full length, and blow the lowest possible note, for a long time. As I feel myself to be running out of breath, I do not stop but continue blowing. I am able to continue blowing the long low note for a very long time, because I have that skill. Finally, though, I need to stop.

Later, I am at a keyboard attempting to transcribe the words for my sister Claire's favorite song, which is "Lord of the Dance." I can hear the song clearly, "Dance, dance, wherever you may be, for I am the Lord of the Dance, said he." Claire's computer screen is set to a very tiny type font, and as I try to type the words of the song into her document, I have to squint to see the tiny letters.

I'm moving through the rooms of a house—a house
party is happening, there are lots of people in each
room talking, drinking, hanging out. I enter a living
room with a double bed in the center. On the bed,
Kate is lying down.

I sit beside Kate—I tell her how sorry I am about
what happened to her daughter. I know that she
knows that my son Sam had died, but now, worse has
happened to her than what had happened to me:
Because she has had two of her children die—first her
son, and now her daughter.

She comforts me about Sam's death, and shows
me her daughter's newborn baby, who she is now
caring for, because her daughter had died.

Her daughter's baby lies on the bed, near her
head. The baby is very tiny—the size of my thumb. It is
wrapped in a bright cloth.

Kate gets up and asks me to look after the baby. I
know that she is doing this to comfort me.

I look into the baby's face, and it is very
beautiful—a newborn, so tiny. I pick it up and it fits
into the palm of my hand. I begin to walk back
through the crowded rooms of the noisy house party,
carefully sheltering the baby in my cupped hands in
front of me, picking my way among the people
partying on the floor. I reach a room where someone
is singing to a group of listeners. It's too loud, so I

turn back, and as I do so, I realize that something has changed with the baby in my cupped hands.

I open my hands and see two pyramidal stones, one white and one black. I am alarmed that the baby has turned into the two stones, but I figure that the stones must be the baby and can also return to being a regular baby—I would just need to enable this to happen.

A man with long hair notices my stones, and asks me why I am confused? He says that this can happen: the stones are Buddha and Jesus.

Now I am holding an earth-globe, and I tell the long-haired man that the globe is bi-polar. He asks my meaning. I say, that just as I hold it by its two sides, so, it has two poles. I say it's not the same meaning as manic-depressive bipolar mind. It's just that the globe has two opposite poles.

I am again clasping the black and white pyramidal stones within my hands, and I begin to retrace my steps back towards the bed, through the crowded party room.

When I get back, Kate is lying on the bed again. As I approach her, ready to explain what happened to the baby, I feel a strange change happening in my hands: it's like bread is rising. I open my hands and see that the baby has been born from the stones. I hand the baby over to Kate, explaining that the baby had turned to black and white pyramidal stones of Buddha and Jesus, but is now reborn as a baby.

Kate seems unsurprised and is glad to have the baby back. She thanks me.

I am high in the mountains, wearing a long robe and a scarf turban around my head: I am a Silk Road traveler, looking down into a valley. Beside me is another man, also in robe and turban.

We are gazing down at a beautiful city with many domed buildings, far below, in the valley. The domes sparkle in sunlight.

The man beside me is my father.

There is a new 4.51% tax on all items we sell at the bookstore. The tax will go directly to Amazon— because the government has decided that everything depends on Amazon, so the tax has been instituted.

I have decided to withhold our store's payment of this tax, like a war-tax protestor. I explain that we are collecting the tax, yes, but we are setting it aside in an escrow account. We are not remitting it.

We will gather other resisters and create a ruckus and protest together.

I am driving a van, like an RV, quickly down an urban highway with lots of traffic around. It's a ring-road that circles a city, with on and off ramps, and I'm in some sort of race or speed contest. I need to swerve off the highway, using an off ramp, and I leap out of the driver's side door, while the van is still moving fast. I am leaping over to another car that's moving alongside—and as I make this move, I turn the wheel of my van-RV so that this vehicle I'm leaving will continue going forward in a curve, across the road.

I jump into the other moving car and get control of it and as I'm driving it away fast, I glance back and see the van-RV I just left is careening across to the far side of the very wide road, and it's now moving up an incline on a side-road. As I drive away from it, I realize that the van-RV is slowing, and is now sliding backwards, down its side-road, and will re-enter the main road backwards, which would be bad and unintended and dangerous.

But I can't deal with this because I am driving the new car away, continuing the race around the highway circling the city.

And now, I need to leap out of the driver's seat of this car into yet a third car, which is now alongside. As I do this, I give a turn to the steering wheel of the car I'm leaving, so that it will move away from the main lane and curve out of traffic—just as I'd done to the original van-RV.

I am now in the third car, and as I glance back, I can see that the first van-RV is still rolling backward, and my second car is curving onward, pretty much as planned, but clearly endangering the general traffic.

I am preparing now to leap from my current, third car, but I am looking all around for anyone who could help with the danger of the earlier abandoned vehicles. I had thought my family, or my staff would be aware of these issues—but no one has noticed my older vehicles and the danger they threaten.

I leap out of the moving third car, allowing it to drive away by itself, and I stand on a hill, and shout "Help!" as loud as possible, trying to attract attention of people who could get to the older vehicles and control them. I continue to shout, "Help!"

I did not have a Bar Mitzvah myself, but I am in charge, as an adult, of making sure that people have Bar Mitzvahs, and the thing about it is that when a young man has a Bar Mitzvah, he has a series of steps, and things that he has to say, that he has to narrate. And it has to be a surprise that when he gets to the point, when he narrates his own death—and it has to be a shock to him when he finds himself in the middle of narrating his own death.

And, the second part of the dream involves, that Amazon has a product where you can buy a Bar Mitzvah, or you can do the Bar Mitzvah through Amazon. And it's, and the part where you're narrating your own death is like a piece of meat, it's like a cherry meat pie.

WHICH WAY UP IS THIS?

There is a little snake, and it says, "I can go straight. I can turn right. I can turn left."

A voice says, "Prove it."

The snake says, "No."

Voice says, "Here is a mirror. Do it in the mirror, to prove it."

Snake says, "I won't."

Voice says, "Show you can go straight, in the mirror."

Snake says, "No."

Voice says, "Go right, in the mirror."

Snake says, "I won't do it."

Voice says, "Show you go left, into this mirror."

Snake says, "No."

WHICH WAY UP IS THIS?

I understand that all reality is a disc rotating at 33 1/3 RPM—like an LP record—it's a Galactic disc—looks like the Milky Way—and that we people emerge from this disc sideways, at a 27 ½ degree angle.

WHICH WAY UP IS THIS?

A woman has a cardboard-colored iPhone-like device—the size of a book—over which she is fitting—pulling down—a tight-fitting flexible diamond net. I think, this stretchy net of diamonds is like Indra's web.

Esme is on a college campus trying to run away because she is forced to live the plot of two picture books. The books are kind of floating in the air. She tells a taxi driver that she will not live the plots of the books.

Later however, she does live several books—

I had arrived at Tobias's house, and I explained: I have Covid, I've been feeling really morbid. But my body is fighting it off, and I'm getting better. My body seems to know what it wants to do for the rest of my life, like: it wants to keep living. And I'm just surprised that my body is so enthusiastic.

And he looked at me with a very stern face, pointed his finger at my face and said, "Be yourself!"

WHICH WAY UP IS THIS?

I am a gnome, and I realize that Fairy Rebecca is in love with me. I feel abashed and joyous. She is smiling at me and flapping her wings and dancing. I realize that I am in love with her too, and I begin to dance also.

In a huge conference hall with a full auditorium a presentation has taken place. A major government project has produced a weapon: it's as big as the fuselage of an airplane. A rolling, stainless steel, bookcase: curved, with lots and lots of shelves. The books are all children's books. I inspect the glowing tailpipe—it is nuclear-powered.

I realize that the books themselves are a mediocre series of conventional merchandise-style books, not quality children's literature. The buyer who has selected these titles is ignorant of the full range of excellent books that should be stocking such a weapon—which after all will be used to overcome an enemy.

I go to a counter and protest that the government entity that has produced this weapon needs to contact the Association of Booksellers for Children or the American Booksellers Association to fix this major problem.

The person at the counter is a functionary who is uninterested and doesn't understand my distinction between the books on the bookcase and the sort of books really needed. But another person behind the counter expresses a bit more interest, although he too is completely ignorant. He points out however that this big rolling bookcase was not produced by the government, so there may not be a way to intervene.

I respond that the conference was held by the Lincoln Imperium—which is not a governmental agency but does have some ideological connection with the government.

I am thinking about the full array of books that ought to be used to effect a change of culture in the nation against whom this huge gleaming rolling nuclear bookcase will be deployed. It is very strange that this has all been centralized and weaponized—I feel that it is misguided and won't work, but if it's going to happen, I should try fix this situation.

Shepherding dad around through a crowded department store—he is in dementia phase and keeps wishing to return to places we have already been. He is looking for some sort of small tool. I think he has imagined this item, but someone else has now located it! It's a sort of pliers with odd wings pointing outwards.

Dad wants to descend some stairs, but they are so steep they're more like a ladder: straight down. I think it's too unsafe for him to go down.

Sam is a toddler who keeps wandering away. I have lost track of him. Perhaps he is sleeping in a pile of coats. But some strangers are now sitting with the coats. When I inquire if they have seen Sam, I see among the pile of coats only a beautiful porcelain doll. That is not Sam. I'm not sure where he has gone.

WHICH WAY UP IS THIS?

I'm interacting remotely—by computer?—with an automated Artificial Intelligence. The AI voice asks me a series of increasingly personal and obscure questions, because it is assembling a password secrecy protocol which will be used by only my closest associates to access my personal secret information if I die. The questions Rebecca and my other family members will be posed after my death are questions only they and I know the answers to.

One question: What is something that happened during your first date only the two of you know? I answer: She accidentally kissed me on the lips when I turned my head.

Another question: What is the last song Rebecca sang with her sister before her sister died? Answer: "Barges."

As the process continues, I realize that the Artificial Intelligence is not only generating a secure protection for my personal information, but it is also attaining the ability to mimic me; it could deceive Rebecca into believing that she is interacting with me, and then it could carry out some nefarious and destructive intention to harm her.

I am walking on the sidewalk with Rebecca and Dad on Ashland Avenue, which is a slightly slanting street, in a version of Chicago a bit like Paris. A very long white luminous limousine is driving slowly alongside us. It is driving so slowly that Dad can open a car door near the front and get in. Rebecca opens a door more towards the center of the limousine and gets in. I am planning to open another door near the rear of the limousine, but by now, although it is going very slowly, it has pulled ahead of me, and I can't catch up to get in.

I am following the white limousine as it proceeds up Ashland Avenue. I am walking rather quickly but can't catch up to it. I phone Rebecca on my cellphone, and we begin to discuss which restaurant we should meet at. They will get out of the limousine there, and I will arrive on foot. We know the city very well, and there are lots of possible restaurants to meet at. We can't decide what kind of food we want to eat. Meanwhile, the limousine is now further ahead from me. I realize that if this were an unfamiliar city, we would have difficulty knowing where to meet, since we wouldn't know the restaurant options.

Ashland Avenue is splitting. This means I am at 26th Street. I think, I need to turn off onto 26th Street. I turn right, onto 26th Street, but almost immediately I realize that it was 29th Street that was the place I should have turned. I go back to Ashland Avenue and continue North.

The white limousine is completely out of sight. I decide to take a shortcut diagonally over to 29th Street, through the park. I leave the road and walk on a path through trees, quickly. My plan is to intercept the limousine ahead, since it will have gone on Ashland Avenue, and then turned left onto 29th Street.

On my head, I have been balancing three luminous white rectangular boxes. They are fragile and stacked on top of one another. Making sure that they don't topple has been something that's slowed me down. But they mustn't break. Two of these boxes will be gifts for Rebecca and dad. I don't know who the third box is for.

From behind a tree, from a shadow, a dark man wearing sunglasses, a tweed jacket, a tie, and tennis shoes, suddenly emerges and approaches me quickly. He is going to attack me. I have no time to react, and I just move at him immediately. Maybe he will stab me and kill me, and the boxes will break, but I cannot avoid him, I plow into him.

I wake up.

We're traveling (in real life): I've had this dream in an airport hotel. I narrate the dream to the real

Rebecca, and she has some ideas about it. A bit later, in the Stockholm airport terminal, as we emerge from security check, I am putting back on my belt. This decorated belt was a gift from Sylvan, my stepson. I look up and see an informational poster on the terminal wall. It is in Swedish. My eye falls on a Swedish word (which I do not know): the word "samlat."

I suddenly realize that the third luminous box in my dream which I was carrying on my head was for my son Sam (Sam Laties).

A young woman has gone on a mission to another land. She is a spy, but with supportive intent, coming from an allied country.

She mingles with a professional group of adults at a lively dinner party. Among these middle-aged and young people, there is a noticeably older man, tall and with white hair. He is in the full confidence of the group—a wise mentor figure.

The visiting young woman feels suspicion that the white-haired confidant is actually a dangerous character with dark intent who is manipulating and exploiting this group of young people.

She is startled to realize that the white-haired man has the power to read her mind, and she knows that he has detected her suspicious thoughts and is right now searching her mind for information about her secret spy mission.

She carries out a defensive maneuver, shutting down her thought process to block his mind-reading intrusion. But even as she does this maneuver, she realizes it is too late: he already carried out his theft of her secret thoughts. She can only hope his success has been partial.

Curtis is standing in front of an easel. He holds a paintbrush. On the paintbrush is a blob of gray-white paint. He is very tall, standing incredibly still, staring at the canvas on the easel. Preparing to paint.

I am thinking, "I thought he was a filmmaker not a painter." But then I recall that he is a painter—I remember this—that first he was a painter and later turned to filmmaking. But first a painter.

And I can't believe how still he is standing as he prepares his brushstroke.

I think the whitish paint was gesso—for a prep layer.

WHICH WAY UP IS THIS?

WHICH WAY UP IS THIS?

I am a member of the cast for a play—we're about to film a segment.

The entire cast had a big party last night—a sort of Thanksgiving Dinner—and the large industrial kitchen that was used to prepare the meal is a complete wreck, with piles of dishes and cooking implements, and lots of leftovers.

There are two sinks, piled in dishes. I need to finish washing these, but I also need to get back over to the set to play my role in the play. Since I haven't memorized my lines, or seen the script, I will just glance at the script rapidly before going on stage. I hope this will be adequate. But now I am trying to wash the dishes.

The faucet head has been replaced by a new-fangled oval head. When I lift the handle to turn the water on, bean soup with chunks of vegetables explodes from the faucet head, spewing at me and in all directions.

I turn the faucet off. Evidently, I will need to learn how to use the new faucet. I go to the other sink, and there too, when I turn on the water, what comes out is this bean-vegetable vomit-like soup, making a mess.

Now I have to wipe the guck off me and get back to the stage set to film the segment.

I'm a member of SNL cast—we have done a series of skits and are in middle of doing a skit in which a man is being courted by another man. The younger man is not enlightened about the nature of the seduction. However, he is encouraged by the side-playing cast members. The sketch concludes when the younger man enters the older man's apartment. The side players address the camera and one of them is licking a lollipop ostentatiously.

I address the camera, and I say, "Three million people are watching this show, and half are shaking their fists, while the other half are cheering us on. But what's important is that we are all here together, aware of one another and having a conversation." Then, another, female cast member chimes in with, "And by the way, this is Andy's last episode with SNL."

The show has concluded and as I walk down a backstage hallway, another female cast member says, "Congratulations! I didn't know you were retiring." When I don't respond immediately, she is embarrassed, and asks, "Did you know?" I say, "Yes, well, I didn't really know, but I had overheard something earlier—but, no, I hadn't been told before." And she responds, "Oh! I'm sorry." Then I say, "No, it's fine, I had been thinking it was around now."

And I wake up thinking, how we play our part for a while, and it didn't start with me, and it won't end with me—it goes on.

I have been working at my laptop on a desk at a café. Very busy. It's on the grounds of my old high school. I haven't been to any of my classes this year, and it's the day before the final class. I was reminded by my sister, passing by, that Mike asked when we will get together to discuss the presentation we're supposed to be making, together, to the class—an English/History class—on the final day of school. We are a team but haven't met all year, and I have attended no classes. (Because I was working on my Schwitters book and ignoring all my class assignments.)

Mike now comes to my desk in the café. I haven't seen him all year. He says, "So, what's going on with us, tomorrow? Do we have a plan?"

I say, "Oh, sorry, I've been working so much on this book—"

He turns and leaves abruptly.

I realize that, actually, I don't even know the name of the teacher, or which classroom it is.

I believe that not only do I have to make this presentation with Mike, but tomorrow there is a final exam.

Also, I have attended none of my other classes.

They would have no choice at the school but to prevent me from graduating.

Can they do that? Would I then attend high school for another year, as a student one year older than everyone else? And what would that be like?

Maybe it would be nice!

But suddenly I realize, oh wow, I can turn this Schwitters book in for my final project for all the classes. They might be unsure, but probably I can persuade them, since the book is such a strong piece, that on its basis, they should let me graduate.

I'm in a car with a middle-aged, dark-haired woman sitting in the passenger seat—but we're reversed—I'm driving, on the right-hand side of the car. Rebecca is in the back seat (I am also driving on the right-hand side of the road). We're in a city which, like San Francisco, has steep hilly roads.

This road I'm driving on has become so steep that it's ninety degrees straight up. I gun the car and keep the pedal all the way down—by dint of sheer energy I revv the car all the way straight up to the next block, where, in the crosswalk, we flatten out entirely.

Rebecca has been excited, in the back seat. The dark-haired woman has been silent and clearly attempting to remain calm. I say, "As long as I don't let up on the pedal, we can do this."

I gun the engine again, and we're heading up the next block—ninety degrees straight up again—up, up, the car goes—and oof we are at the next intersection flattened out safely again.

There are only two more blocks of these ninety-degree streets to go. I check around—Rebecca and the dark-haired woman are not saying anything, and I just go for it, pedal to the metal—revv, and we're going straight up the road again—revving without a let up until—there, we're flattened out at the cross-street again.

Now there's only one more block of this to do. I just go for it, the pedal against the car floor, we're going straight up, the engine is performing surprisingly well but I'm glad this is the last one—up, up—and we're there, flat on the top of the hill.

We have arrived at a fancy hotel-restaurant. Waiters and staff are laughing and cheering us. The dark-haired woman gets out of the car and stumbles over to the restaurant. Rebecca is laughing. She gets out of the car, and I pick her up in my arms. I realize that she is naked under her dress and I am cradling her naked bottom. She is smiling and giggling and kissing me.

I think, well—this restaurant looks kind of expensive, but I guess I can put it on a credit card—we certainly aren't going to look around in town right now for somewhere else. And the view is incredible.

I am carrying her down some steps towards where there are tables overlooking the city.

There's a girl who I'm in this folktale with, I'm seeing over her shoulder.

The girl is receiving some introductory lessons—maybe she's eleven or twelve years old—into how to become a healer. And the lesson is with an older woman.

So, it's a village, and she's just going to be engaged in helping to heal the sick, in her village. And she understands that of course it's a process of communing with the other world, because when people are sick, their spirits are in a conditional state, relative to the visible world.

And so she's just begun to get some healing training, in a sort of hospital hut. And the woman who's the leading healer of the village is called away. And says to the girl, "Okay, you just try to take my place for the short while I'm gone."

So just then, the older healer who's teaching her has left, and the girl of eleven or twelve feels that, "Oh, this is a great responsibility, I'm not really ready for this—I don't know what will happen."

Just then, she hears a cry, from a hut maybe across the village compound. And she realizes that it's coming from the direction of her own hut. So she rushes across the compound, and as she comes to her own hut, she realizes it was her mother, who has been taken ill all of a sudden.

And as she enters her hut, she sees that her mother has collapsed onto the ground and there's another unfamiliar woman dressed in white who is standing there with a serious look on her face. And she (the girl) understands that this other woman is a spirit who has come from the other world to take her mother's soul. Her mother has had a heart attack and is lying on the ground, and this other spirit is standing there, very serious. She (the girl) knows that at that moment, this girl is going to have to try to prevent this death-character from taking her own mother's soul. Her mother is middle-aged, and no-one expected her to die.

So, the girl, her first thought, she goes up to the Spirit of Death, and tries to address her, and says, "Don't take my mother's soul."

And the Spirit of Death is dismissive and says, "I'm going to take her right now."

And then the girl realizes that simply being direct with the Spirit of Death won't work. So, she decides to try to bargain with Death, to leave her mother alive. And she says, "Well, is there something that I can do, that will appease you?"

And the Spirit of Death says, "Now don't try to bargain with me, I'm going to take your mother right now. She's going to die right now, I'm about to take her soul."

And the girl realizes that she doesn't know what to do, and how to engage with the Spirit of Death to make a deal.

At this point—there's been some awareness in the village that this is happening. At this point another, much older, wise woman comes into the hut and kind of gestures for the girl to stand back. And she, the older woman, goes over to the Spirit of Death and speaks to her in a very low voice. And the Spirit of Death and the older woman go over to a low table and begin to have some tea together.

At that point, shortly afterwards, the Spirit of Death leaves, and goes away.

And the girl's mother comes out of her collapse on the ground and recovers from the heart attack.

A little bit later, the girl manages to go up to the old woman who had successfully negotiated with Death, and says, "What did you say to her? How did you convince her to go away?"

And the old woman says, "Well, what I did was I asked her if in some way the village had offended her. And if that was why she had decided to take this healthy middle-aged victim. And the Spirit of Death revealed to me that, yes, she had been offended by the village. And then," the old woman continues, "I asked well—I'm so sorry that this happened. The village had no intention of offending you, could you please tell us what we did to cause you to take offense?"

"And the Spirit of Death said, 'Well, I was in the process of taking a very old member of your group whose time it was to die, and who was ready to go, and I was interfered with by your village—there was a particular person who cursed me, and attempted to send me away, and vilified me. And so, to punish your tribe for this behavior towards me, I decided, I'll take somebody who's in good health, and who has importance and use to your group, just to show you that you can't behave that way towards me. So, I picked somebody—I picked this woman—whose time wasn't come yet—just to show you.'"

And then, the woman had said to the Spirit of Death, "Oh, well that person who behaved that way towards you, we all know her, and she's a fool. We understand that other woman was ready to die, and we're so sorry that you were treated with disrespect, and we will speak to her and ask her to amend her ways, and certainly we would not stand in your way of taking someone whose turn it was to die."

"And then the Spirit of Death was consoled, and appeased, and said, 'All right, if you will treat me with due respect, in the other case, then I will not take this woman. Thank you for your correct understanding of my role.'"

"And that's how I caused the Spirit of Death to leave your mother at this time."

And so, the young woman, who was just starting her lessons learned this lesson, and her mother was saved as well.

I was helping to run an elaborate conference—sort of an academic conference with many different sessions in different rooms going on simultaneously. There were a lot of different colleges in the area which had collaborated on this conference, but it wasn't run by any one of the colleges. So, there were students and faculty from all these different colleges who were all present in this conference center.

And the students were all—there were tables of food, kind of, in the eating rooms, and the students were having a lot of fun, and was kind of a mess, cause there was food that was spilled onto the floor. And the eating period was coming to a conclusion, and there were sessions that were going into session in all of these rooms off of these main entertainment areas, and there was a particular session that I had— oh—Rebecca's sister had been there, along with some other people and she had a tuba.

And I had encouraged her—we had come upon a theater full of—no—a dining table that was full of people dressed in marching band uniforms. And I had encouraged Rebecca's sister to—because she was also wearing a marching band uniform on her own, or, some kind of uniform—I'd encouraged her to hang out with these people in their marching band uniforms, because she had a tuba—so she had gone with them into their session, and I'd heard the sound of improvisation, and I'd looked in, and she was improvising on her tuba—very vigorously, along with the other marching band performers. So, I thought, ok that worked out well.

And then I had looked in on another session, which was kind of a touchy-feeling kind of Buddhist tantra transcendental talk which was being given by a sort of guru character who I was a bit suspicious of. And I had got them started and I went away, and I came back, and I saw that just as I suspected, they were all having an orgy. They had lined themselves up, they were all naked, and they had lined themselves up in some sort of complicated pattern to start having sex.

And I shouted at them, "Put your clothes on! Break it up. This is an academic conference. This is ridiculous."

And everyone was annoyed with me, but they kind of understood that they were in fact violating the ethics of the conference. And I said, "If you don't get your clothes back on, I'm gonna call the cops, right now." And I was especially annoyed at the fellow who was you know, the leader of this session, who was this sort of guru character. And he looked very irritated with me, he certainly felt threatened, that I warned I was gonna call the cops. So I said, "Ok, I'm gonna go away right now, but when I come back, I expect everybody to be completely dressed. Because this is ridiculous, you're completely unethical."

So, I left, but then I thought, "They're not gonna get their clothes back on."

So, then I went back, and indeed they were all still lying there. So, I said, "Get your clothes back on! I'm gonna—I'm not gonna call the cops, but I'm gonna stand here until you do."

So, then they all were getting up, and I said, "This is absolutely ridiculous. This is not at all what you think it is. This is a complete fraud. The truth is—"

And then I started giving this lecture about reality. And I said, "You're completely deluded. You think that your body is something that you can make some use of but in fact, there is no distinction, you don't— you can't USE your body. You don't HAVE a body." And I said, "You think that your hand is like a fork, that you can pick something up with. That's ridiculous! You don't HAVE a hand. This is an illusion. You shake your hand and you"—and I slapped my hand, and I said, "This is just an illusion. Clearly you know that the fork is composed of particles and surely you realize that your hand is composed of particles, but that is ridiculous. Every particle is simply a concatenation of energies. And the energies are just— when you slap your hand it's just energies resisting energies. And you can't cause energies to go away—

even if your hand were completely to dissolve, then, what would happen to them?"

And then somebody—a woman—said, "The energy would still be energy!"

And I said, "Exactly! The energy just becomes a cloud of energy! Your hand can never go away. Your body can never go away. Because there is no 'your body'—you ARE your body. You are the cloud of energy. And even if was apparently dissipating, it would still be persistent. So, you can never be anything but what you are. And you don't have to engage in these kinds of practices where you think you're going through a transformation or you're losing yourself. You don't HAVE yourself; you ARE yourself. You ARE your body."

At this point, this guru guy seemed to have been mollified. And now he was trying to curry favor with me, and he came up to me with a plate with some cake on it, and a fork. And he said, "Thank you for calling me a master." And he handed me this, and I was very irritated that he was kind of trying to salvage his reputation by currying favor with me, and I took the plate with the cake, but I put it down.

I'm in a small sailboat, on the wide-open ocean,
blue sky, the sunset in the distance. I am sailing
towards an island, which rises up larger and larger as
I approach. It has a sheer cliff face and I'm sailing
directly toward this many-colored cliff face. I can see
that there is a sort of map of the world on the cliff
face—and the continents seem very active and alive.
But it's definitely a rock face. However, as I sail
towards this island with its cliff face, I intend to sail
directly against the cliff. I hope that I will be able to
sail right into the cliff, and thus, enter the world.

I wake up (I didn't actually sail into the cliff), and I
think of the William Blake proverb from Hell: "Eternity
is in love with the productions of time." I do feel that
my dream image involved me sailing in eternity and
desiring to enter time/the-world. Like being born.

Intricate movie-like plot—a sort of fantasy sequence. With my sisters I have transported complex jeweled objects out of the past—we have obtained—or extracted—dozens of these crown-like things. Now we are concerned to conceal these, but also to photograph them for documentation. As each crown is photographed, I can see that many other people are secretly observing, via a complex setup of mirrors that reflect into each other. Even at a great distance there are people, in distant buildings, down hallways, on rooftops, watching us photograph these jewels, by utilizing the spying mirrors.

I feel like the jewels would be safer from theft if they were returned into the past. However, I can see that while we are all comfortable in this present, that were we to be transported to the past, our lives would be immediately transformed to dangerous and troubled. And the crowns can't be returned to the past unless accompanied by a person. So—that's not a good choice.

Meanwhile, there are threats of capture: adversaries are trying to steal the jewels.

I awaken; I've been lying on a daybed in a bright, white-walled room. It must be in our house in Easton. Sarah, Curtis and Otis are there, seated. Rebecca is also there. They are chatting.

I ask what is going on. Sarah looks at me with exasperation and distress. I realize that—I really should already know exactly what has taken place. I must have been part of this decision-making, which led to Sarah and Curtis being out here with Rebecca and me. I think, "I'm in dementia now. I can't remember things that I have already been told." I am powerfully curious—but I know I must have already been told—and I'm just annoying people by asking again.

WHICH WAY UP IS THIS?

Saturday, September 23 (my 64th birthday).

The extended family (1990s, including my parents, and my sisters and their children) has been on a group vacation in Japan—and this final day in Toyko we had split up to do different things.

My mother was set to take Sam (aged about nine years old) and two of his boy cousins on a day of tourist activities, including a visit to the Tu Fu house—a historical house where Tu Fu (the Chinese poet) had once lived—because Sam wanted to visit there—as well as to a video-game gallery (for one of the nephews)—and to another stop for another nephew. I am worried and doubtful that my mother is capable of carrying off this detailed plan, but—I can't stop it from happening, and I head off for my own complex day of activities—which unfold in a gigantic crowded urban shopping mall.

Now it is the end of the day, and Sam, with my mother and the nephews had returned, and were eating at a food court, which I noticed from a distance.

They and the rest of the extended family have gone outside to pile into a mini-bus or a van which will be taking us all to the airport to fly home from our Japan trip.

I am running around before joining them in the van—trying to tie up loose ends, make sure nobody left anything behind. I don't have any pants on, which is kind of embarrassing, but I don't let that slow me down.

I see, on the bench in the food court—where I'd noticed, before, Sam was sitting—that there's some stuff. I hurry over there, and at his seat there is a small pile of banknotes and a coin. Looking closely, I see that one of these banknotes is a Tu Fu banknote. This is about the size of a coupon, very thin—maybe like rice-paper—translucent, slightly green tinted, with very light printing, in red or pink. It's so beautiful, and delicate. I figure Sam bought it as a souvenir of his visit to the Tu Fu house earlier in the day—he must have bought these other few banknotes and the coin at the same time.

I get out my wallet, and carefully place the items into my brown leather wallet, which is already jammed with my scraps of papers, and which bulges, so that it's hard to be sure that the new items won't get warped—but, the Tu Fu banknote is so small that it does fit in fine.

Sam now appears—he has left the mini-bus and run back to the food court because he'd realized that he'd forgotten his souvenirs from the Tu Fu house. He asks me if I have found his Tu Fu things.

I show him how I have just now put them carefully into my wallet for safekeeping.

There are several young people wearing black t-shirts with a logo imprinted on them.

Above in the sky, two angels are pissing—the yellow piss goes down to earth and soaks the young people's t-shirts.

I am watching this—as the young people are annoyed, and I say to them, "It's all about how you see it." This statement causes the angels overhead to begin pissing brightly colored paint colors, which land on the t-shirts and spatter them brightly with colors.

The young people are delighted, and dance around in the spilling colors.

I'm in the passageway of a medieval city like Kathmandu with shops filled with traditional weaving and cloth, but I'm rushing towards a square—I'm involved with running some festival—in the square a tall man is leading a ritual with a large crowd. As I rush behind him, across the square, towards another passageway—I notice that he has next to him a basket piled high with shiny metal trumpets. They're like Tibetan trumpets—a sort of medieval instrument, with lots of crooks and bends in the horn.

The preacher-guy and I know each other. He makes a side-comment to me—urging me to grab a trumpet, which he's about to pass out to the congregation, and join in playing. He knows I play this sort of instrument.

But I make an excuse—I'm needed to operate the festival—so I have to rush onward.

WHICH WAY UP IS THIS?

Underground caverns:

1) With director of museum who is interviewing me—I will be marketing director for new underground museum—she wants any notes I took about what a guy said during a previous walkthrough last year—I'm not sure I kept my notes / Several of us are excited that we'll be a team doing this launch, but I wonder privately what our salaries will be—

2) I eat a sort of translucent gelatinous fruit of the underground cavern.

3) I converse will an odd man—strange accent and clothes—I ask a worker if there are Orthodox Jews down here—then I'm going with the odd man deeper— he is heading back to his home—there are a different branch of human species deep underground—they escaped thousands of years ago—from persecution— diverged genetically—but I am related to them—as a modern Jew.

4) There are also Mythical Iranians in another underground enclave—I learn this from the Orthodox Jew.

Hosting an author event for Madeleine L'Engle. I tried to get one or another professor attending to do the interview with her but realize I've failed to line someone up so I must do it myself. I introduce her saying the things I know about her—based on being in Chicago / home of ALA.

1) She is very concerned with Love—central to her work with children.

2) She loves to travel.

3) She cares deeply about community (someone calls out What do you mean? And I explain Togetherness.)

4) She is deeply religious as a Christian and her address was St. John's Cathedral.

I tell how at her 1986 event at my bookstore she was followed in by dozens of admirers.

During my rather rapid, but smooth introduction, I'm exchanging glances with her—this is the prelude to our interview.

Sarah and I are together after returning from a lengthy, complex trip to Zanzibar. She is sixteen, and a lot older than when we went there. She'd been twelve when we'd left, and so—so much has happened since we left.

I remind her how she'd been anxious, before we'd gone. But that since so much has happened, and all the things she was worried about have been replaced by what actually did happen—perhaps she would like to write a letter now, speaking to her twelve-year-old self—and saying things that might be what she would like to tell her twelve-year-old self, from the perspective of her older self.

We then feel worried about Sam. He has been out in the town—and we're not sure he got back safely. Since we're in a sort of hotel or dormitory building, we run downstairs to a group bunk-bed room where he has his bed. At first, we don't see him, but then we do see him, sprawled out on an upper bunk in the corner. We go over to him and tell him how glad we are that he got back from town safely.

He says that he likes to be out in the city in the middle of the night, because everything is happening—there is action, and it's very real—that's why he goes out at night. He seems happy with how things went, but also, he wants to sleep now.

Curtis is a big aficionado of the Ancient Greek filmmaker Aristarchus. Curtis is really fascinated with Aristarchus's editorial technique, which you can assess by examining the physical artifacts: the films themselves show where they were cut and spliced.

Crouching in a cat-like position is my old girlfriend.
She has a see-through top, and her breasts hang
down—very sexy posture. Her bottom is swathed in a
heavy white cloth, like a diaper. I'm passing through
the room, and I'm trying to avert my gaze—I don't
want to leer at her breasts, but I see them out of the
corner of my eyes. I'm hoping she stays in this part of
the room, because I am crossing to the kitchen sink,
where my wife is dressed in an apron, doing dishes.

I approach my wife—she begins to complain to me.
I'm attempting to parry her attacks—she is anxious
and upset—I am to blame for her unhappiness, and
she is detailing this. Meanwhile she's vigorously
washing dishes. I particularly don't want her to notice
that my old girlfriend is crouching in her sexy outfit
just in the next room. I know my wife will be jealous
that I'm still seeing my old girlfriend—who is sort of my
mistress—although my ex-girlfriend is uncontrollable
and unpredictable....

My ex-girlfriend is now crawling towards where
I'm enduring my wife's complaints. I try gesturing—
please do not come over where you will be seen. But
my ex-girlfriend is really going to come over here.
She looks at me with defiance, and suddenly says,
"I'm fucking her!"

Suddenly my wife is sitting hoisted up on top of the
counter with her dress up, and my ex-girlfriend's face

is immersed in my wife's crotch. My wife's face is totally transformed—she's having an orgasm.

I'm stunned. Evidently my ex-girlfriend and my wife have been having an affair?! This is happening in front of me? I feel a surge of jealousy that my wife is getting my ex-girlfriend's attention.

I'm also shocked—but relieved—that my wife has stopped whining at me.

And, I wonder, am I invited to join them? Maybe I could enter my ex-girlfriend from behind—except, she has this big white diaper on and I'm not sure I could get it off!

And anyhow, it's possible that their blatant sexual engagement is specifically a refusal of me—that the two of them are intentionally banishing me, in hooking up together.

I'm having lunch at a restaurant with Peter. He's quite pleasant and genial. I am kind of playing up to him—he retains some sort of authority. Although he damaged my life and destroyed my business, he's just a corporate CEO who never got emotionally involved. So, we're having a pleasant lunch.

He's left the children's museum, and he says he's taken a position at The Stuart [an art history museum]. I comment that, in that case, he'll be working with Nick. But Peter is a bit taken aback—he doesn't know who Nick is.

Nick is a positive person, in my life—and I don't feel like trying to prepare Peter for working with Nick or being involved in introducing them to each other.

Now—I am in a museum and along with a lot of people I'm examining an exhibition of huge, blown-up photographs, framed on the walls. They are in black and white. They depict crowd scenes—from my youth when I was at Yale. One is a photo of a party—lots of people are on the ground embracing. I recognize the party—and I see that I'm actually there, in the photo, on a mattress on the ground among lots of people. I look so much younger than I look today.

I also examine other huge black-and-white group photos in which I appear as one among dozens of people. For instance, at a protest rally.

I glance away, looking at all the viewers who've come to see this exhibition.

Then, I return my attention to the photographs. To my perplexity, there are now fewer people in the photos, and the people in these seem to have changed places. I myself am absent from scenes where I just saw myself. These photos are transforming.

I realize that many of the museumgoers are clustered around a woman with curling black hair, who is intoning a poem or spell, which causes an iPhone that's by her feet to glow with spiral patterns. It must be this incantation which is causing the photographs to transform.

I have the feeling that the entire process is actually causing the past itself to transform.

I speak up. I tell the shaman-figure that I cannot accept this. My father raised me not to believe in this sort of thing.

She has lost concentration because of me, and on coming out of her trance, she speaks to me with annoyance. "What did your father teach you?"

I search for words. "He was a scientific rationalist."

She doesn't know what this amounts to. "A materialist?"

I try to clarify: "A positivist. Yes, a materialist."

She is irritated. "I grew up in a wasteland of fast food and broken-down cars, trauma and victimization. I had to escape this pointless, empty landscape of my life." It was out of this youth that she became a shaman.

I'm completely sympathetic. "I agree—the outcomes of materialistic beliefs have been disastrous for society."

However, I feel, more than this, that my father's stance of waiting for scientific clarity on any question, and of refraining from thought about issues on which no mainstream scientific consensus existed, had left him disengaged—

Now I see that the shaman is naked, and, although a woman, has male genitals.

Image of a book jacket. It's a green, paperback book.

On this book jacket is a person—a woman – holding a book, face forward.

I can see that the book jacket depicted is the same book—it's a picture of the very same book, with the woman holding it.

Looking more closely, I see that on the jacket of the book within the book, is the same picture, getting tinier and tinier.

Infinite regress.

I'm dealing with a toilet tank as large as a
swimming pool. My own shit is floating in the water—a
huge amount. I'm in the pool, trying to clean the shit.
Sam is there too. There's a grinder—a sort of disposal
in the bowl of a toilet, next to the pool/tank itself. I'm
stuffing shit down this toilet bowl. Sam (aged about
five) is interested in a handle which, when turned,
causes the grinder to spin and grind up the shit. I
keep packing shit in, and Sam keeps turning the
handle and grinding it, but there's always more. The
toilet bowl can be filled up, and the grinder can
dispose of the shit but then I have to pack more in.

Up from the bottom of the toilet bowl, out of the
grinder comes a gleaming, copper/rainbow slinky. A
spiral of metallic spring. This slinky is about eight
inches across—it's an unusually large one. Like any
slinky, it's kind of relaxed, however, it's getting
larger; it keeps emerging.

I think: are all slinkies made from shit, like this? It's
so shiny and clean! How could something so shiny
and clean come from shit? Is that gross? It seems like
that means slinkies must be gross.

I am talking with the manager of a fancy restaurant in a conference center. He's telling me he just learned that a large party of people are coming soon to the restaurant. At the center of this group are two celebrities, who were matched up together on a blind date. They are Patti Smith and Jason Momoa.

The word is, they did not hit it off, however, they did go through with the whole exercise, and after their day of recreation (with all their friends and hangers-on), they will all be coming here for dinner.

This manager seems a bit exasperated—however, he has things under control. He says that he's of course going to have to comp all the food, but he is definitely going to charge for drinks: the sale of the drinks should cover the expenses.

He tells me that during the day, all these people went to a recreational activity called "Runway." It's a new fad. You go to a flat place out in the desert, and these souped-up cars and buggies and trucks are out there. People get in and drive crazily and dare each other to hit them—like bumper cars. It's totally out of control. It started in Nevada, but then spread to other states, and now it's in thirty-five states.

The Ardmore-Stollman dream involves an edition of an ancient ethnic text called—was a philosopher named Ardmore, with editorial work by Stollman. And the text was edited by Stollman in a way such as to cull phrases or aphorisms from the larger text. Such as to selectively alter the full thrust of the meaning of the ancient text.

And the other editorial material was—ok the Hazel-Nancy part of the dream, there was a character named Hazel, a television character, who would appear briefly during *Captain Kangaroo* shows just before the commercials. And with a little child, and Hazel was the maid—Hazel was always—what happened in these little episodes, which were recurrent—every day in *Captain Kangaroo*—was that there would have been some kind of misfortune or mishap, and Hazel would make a pithy aphoristic commentary and then kind of cock her eyebrow.

And there was an editor—Nancy—who went through all these original episodes and cut them—edited them—from the archive—either first went through and removed most of them, and later removed all of them. And these had been recently—this editorial work had been reassessed.

And the woman who originally played Hazel was now a very old actress and it was now decades later. But there had been a compilation made of all the original, sort of, aphoristic moments and they revealed the kind of social mores of the early 1960s that were now completely rejected by the society, and it was sort of embarrassing for the actress to have been making sexist and patriarchal lessons for this little child.

And these both happened in the context of my visit to this gigantic bookstore, which was Veronica's bookstore Word Up, which had grown and grown. And it was so large now that it occupied the extended ground floor of a former industrial space. And it was a combination new and used bookstore with all these different sections.

And I had gone there because there was a talk followed by a musical concert in an afternoon. And at first not that many people had come, but then more and more people had come, and then the music had started. And the bookstore had become so—it was like—it was such an incredible community space—there were so many people, and it was so warm and positive and creative—I was stunned by the fabulous inventory and the amazing energy there, and the terrific staff—and at some point, Veronica herself was like moving through this crowd, and she was completely unnoticed. And she'd been running this place and growing it and keeping this incredibly low profile the whole time. I was just so impressed.

I have been involved in producing a festival. I'm on my cell phone, walking through a crowded street talking to a publicist or a marketing person or a reporter, who tells me there's been an announcement from the city of an emergency. Since the festival is just about to launch, and there's all these tables in the streets and events are being set up inside of a number of storefronts and performance spaces along the street, it's very late to try to respond to an emergency. But this reporter is saying they were just about to publish and to start releasing information, but the city has just announced an emergency, so everything should go on hold. And they can't publish the information.

So, I say, well, it's true that there's been some alert issued about a potential emergency, but it's not clear that something is really going to happen. And nobody knows what really this is about, whether it's weather, or some kind of terrorist threat, or what's going to happen, so I think they should just publish the information and just assume that everything's going to be fine.

So, then I'm off the phone and I'm in a sort of loft, where a theatrical production is being set up, and there's a lot of people around.

And I see a man who looks somewhere between Jack Nicholson or a movie star from the 1950s. Sort of medium build with a squarish face and he's wearing a shirt that's splotched as if he'd been painting and splashing paint around—maybe like a Jackson Pollock-splashed paint. And he's got this sort of demented look on his face.

And I realize that he is the serial killer, who's on the loose. And was the cause of this emergency announcement. And I'm seeing him right in front of me. And I know that his plan is to kill a whole bunch of people.

So, I kind of move towards him, to try to grapple with him, and he moves towards me, and I realize I could get killed, and I call out, "I love my son Sam!" because it's like my last words. And I realize I could be misunderstood as saying "Son of Sam" as if this guy is the Son-of-Sam serial-killer. So, I'm confused about whether I should say, "I love Sam and Sarah!"

But anyway, he runs—instead of fighting me, he escapes, and he runs past me, and off down the street.

So, then I turn and I run after him, through all sorts of constructions, like stage constructions, and table set-ups—through this festival—and I lose sight of him, and then I'm kind of wandering through another of these crowded rooms with a bunch of people setting stuff up for performances.

And then I see him again. And I try to confront him again, but there's a stack of picture books, which he is pushing towards me to keep me away from him, but I grab—I put my arms around him and I grab him. And I've got him in a sort of grip.

And then I realize that he's got a hammer, and he's using the back side of the hammer, behind his back—his hands are behind his back and he's got this hammer and he's using the edge of the hammer to sort of pry my fingers off of where I've got his arms pinned around his back. And the stack of picture books is still sort of between us, so our bodies aren't really touching.

And I have a sort of view of the two of us from the side. And we look very much alike. But he's got this sort of really nasty grimace and he's bald. And I have very little hair also. (It's like "Evil Bruce Willis" versus "Good Bruce Willis.")

So, we're sort of twins locked in this grip like a Sumo-wrestler grip.

And I call, "Help! Help!" And I need somebody to come and assist me and I'm really calling, "Help! Help!"

And at this point I realize that Rebecca is poking me, and that I've been calling "Help!" out loud from sleep—and I wake up.

WHICH WAY UP IS THIS?

128

Rebecca and I have been climbing a mountain—it's rocky and steep, and we're in a ravine. We're clambering up this ravine, and it begins to snow like crazy—the mountainside is covered with snow and it's very hard to keep climbing.

We aren't really alone—this is a popular climbing area and there are lots of other people out here climbing. But we can't see anyone else now that it's snowing so hard. I'm beginning to think we'd better give up and return to the last lodge—which is quite a ways behind us.

Just at that moment there's a fierce wind, and the snow blows aside to reveal a staircase in the side of the mountain. We struggle onto it and climb up it.

Now we are at a lodge, in the mountain. Maybe we got there by the stairs. It's very crowded with other climbers. It's warm inside, but through the windows the snowstorm is blowing hard outside. Rebecca heads through the lobby back towards bedroom areas of the lodge, but there are clearly no empty beds. I go to the front desk, and request to rent a room for the night.

The hotel desk clerk speaks to me in French. He says I should of course have reserved several months in advance like everyone else.

I ask him if there is really nothing for us? Here we are, and we cannot leave after all, because of the storm.

He says that for one night it will be "Neuf Cent"— that is, nine hundred dollars. I think, "Ah—there really is an empty room available." So, I say, "So expensive?"

He repeats that if one asks at the last minute, of course one will have to pay full price.

I think, "Could I manage to pay nine hundred? Maybe I should do it."

I now have a room—where Eli Salver appears as my assigned roommate.

Eli is the boss of something that I'm not involved with, and he has his own boss, who I am aware of. Eli is short-tempered and unpleasant, but I try to make the best of it. After all, I do have this room—it's really my room and he is my roommate.

Second part of dream: Eli Salver is arguing with his girlfriend. They're in line outside the supermarket. They're both wearing grey terrycloth bathrobes. They're both quite tall. It's as if they've just had sex and now, they're outside the grocery store in line, but still in their bathrobes. They seem oblivious to everyone around them. Just arguing with each other loudly.

The girlfriend is quite mad at Eli. She's a very brassy woman, with a long face. She evidently had to leave the country, and then come back in, to renew a visa and get her papers in order. It was a huge hassle for her. But Eli is a super-busy guy and isn't caring. He is the boss of something or other—he has other worries than hers.

But she is yelling about her predicament, and she wants his full involvement.

I have arrived at this grocery store just now, to join this line outside—I'm pulling my little green metal wagon. Eli is my roommate. He was assigned to the same dorm room with me, and so far he's been a very unpleasant roommate, very brusque and stand-offish. The girlfriend was around a little bit, but she left. I wasn't aware she was back in town.

Now I say to them, "Gonna fill up our refrigerator!" gesturing in a jolly way to my empty cart.

Eli barely glances at me—he waves his hand as if to say, "Go away"—and he continues in his argument with the girlfriend.

But the girlfriend looks at me and seems to acknowledge me slightly more—she does understand that they will be hungry and will want the food I'm going to buy. But she hasn't stopped in her berating of Eli, even though she does nod to me.

I say, "You youngsters! I have seen it all—this problem is not a big deal. What I've been through—divorce, business collapse, my son's death—your problem is not much!"

They are ignoring me entirely.

I am Katana (a shamanic skeleton-guy). Trying to get my own costume at last minute, for the party/festival/performance.

I've decided on a skeleton face mask. It's a hard-plastic, high quality skull mask that fits over the head.

Two sales guys are at a register. They gesture upward to where lots of costume-masks are hanging on strings from the ceiling. The skeleton-mask is not among the hanging masks displayed though.

I also wonder: What would I wear to look like a skeleton? Gonna seem cheesy to wear a sheet—I don't have any other idea.

Before this scene—I was told to dust my outfit with purple paint-dust, but the shop has none. I ask what about blue? The salesperson said no, that won't stick. I will have to go with orange paint dust, because that does stick. Although I don't really want to be painted orange.

Before that—I have been organizing an event—I'm wearing sandals, but I ought to go back for boots—I'm told by a woman to do this—because the mud will get worse, and my sandals will just sink in the mud.

Rebecca and I have been involved with a performance series or school—we are now in a room having a conversation with a tall, older man with white hair. He is a teacher—very engaged and very concerned about matters now unfolding

But then we find ourselves chatting with some characters in a different plane of reality. From their standpoint, the earlier scene is of little concern—because they themselves are like gods who incarnate into situations like the earlier scene. The white-haired teacher man is unaware that he is really a sort of human incarnation of one of the gods. So—these god-creatures themselves are very relaxed—and it's a bit amusing to them how seriously the people living in that human world take themselves.

A lengthy, violent dream like a Star Wars movie, with lots of plot twists, double-cross characters—lying and cheating, and murders.

After the plotted part, a scene where a teen with a gun is in a bookstore or classroom with Beth P., the teacher. Beth is at a blackboard with twenty-five chalked-up squares on the board. The guy is asking her some illogical questions—he's clearly disturbed and unpredictable. Beth is amiable and pleasant, and although it's still the middle of the day, she begins to turn off lights, gets her coat, and tells him, "I'm closing up now! Thanks for stopping by."

She manages to leave the room, with him trailing behind her. She rapidly gets out of the building, to her car, and has escaped.

I am the manager of a bookstore on a college campus and it's a very busy day. The store is on several different levels, it's lodged inside of an old building and the bookshelves are packed with books and also toys, especially, glowing figurines, which I've got from a new supplier.

And there's a lot of people shopping, and I'm moving through the rooms of the bookstore. And I'm a pretty new manager, but I have implemented my own rearrangement of the merchandise. And I'm kind of moving back towards where the receiving area is, where there's a back loading dock with parking lot behind it. To try to make sure I can get boxes in smoothly to be received and put out on the floor. And I've gone down some steps.

And in one of the rooms, I've reworked with lots of additional toys—there's a guy there who's also new at the college that owns the bookstore. And he is the new history librarian, librarian of the history section.

And I need to go down the steps further, to the back entrance. But now I've got to push aside, because there's this whole crowd of prisoners, Black men, in sort of work clothes, being ushered in through this back door, and they seem kind of dangerous but also beaten down and worn out. So, I just try to stay out of the way.

And there's this one boy, a Black teenage boy, who has been kind of hanging around the history library, down the steps from the bookstore, for several years, and he's kind of like a star pupil in a local school. And everyone's very hopeful that he's gonna be successful, but it's kind of unnerving that he's there—he's been down at the history library just down the steps—when these older Black men coming from the prison work crew are coming through. And so, there's some anxiety that he might be depressed, or thrown off his academic ladder by seeing this discouraging example of what could happen to you when you grow up and you're Black.

Anyway, the work crew manages to sort of squeeze through up the steps past me, and past us, the history librarian guy and the young Black student.

And then I'm going downstairs into the history library. And it's an unusual library because it has all these sculptural figurines, with military paraphernalia like tanks and guns, and also battle scenes, all depicted in plaster, like plaster of Paris. And it's also a gift shop, and I begin to think, "Boy, this is just the kind of thing that Sam would like." And I could buy him one of these battle scenes as a gift, a sort of military scene—because he was very into military history.

And the military historian is down there too, in his library with all these battle sculptures. And he's kind of puttering around, and I realize that Sam is there, doing research. And Sam is kind of examining some books and also, he's looking carefully at some of these military sculptures. And I'm trying to decide what one he would really love to own. But he seems to be very engaged with his studies. So, I think I'm not going to bother him. I'd just like to decide what gift to give him.

Meanwhile the military historian is also down there, kind of puttering around, and there's a couple of adults there who are just at the college for the day. And they've come down also from the gift shop into this military history library and the military historian is showing them, and also me, this manuscript which was donated by some wealthy donor to the college and who specializes in donating to this historical library. And this manuscript is on display. And it's lit up, it's a scroll that's kind of lit up, and so we're looking at this scroll and he's explaining how he's renaming the library after these donors, and they're very generous but you can't control what they're going to donate. They don't usually give money; they'll donate some very valuable artifact and then he has to figure out some way to display it.

And then I'm going out from the military library because it's nearing the end of the day and I have to go back to the dormitory along with these two people—and probably they're Lee and Eric, two professors who are sort of visiting another college. Because it's sort of an alumni reunion weekend.

And now I seem to have switched from being the manager of the bookstore to being a returning alumnus who's been kind of puttering around campus going to the various activities for the returning alums. And I'm talking to Lee and Eric in a kind of dispassionate way about the new parking policies at the college.

And then the military historian is there too, he's kind of left work, and he's asking for advice about what he should say to patrons of the military library when they come and ask him for information about the new parking rules for the college. Cause he knows that the parking is really complicated, and he doesn't really understand it, but people are always asking him about where they should park, and how much it will cost.

And Lee and Eric and I—we know what the parking rules are but it takes so long to explain them that we look at each other—and I say, "Well, just tell them it costs a quarter an hour," and Eric says, "Tell them they should try to park in one of the lots near the college," and then we're all kind of attempting to go on our way so we don't get stuck talking with this military librarian.

And I'm crossing the campus, but I can't remember where the dorm room is for the returning alumni. And then I see Rebecca coming from a different direction. She and I had split up at the beginning of the day because we were going to different programs, and she's coming towards me, and she has tears in her eyes. And I say, "Are you all right?"

And I can tell that she knows where our dorm is, and it's a building that's quite close to us, and there's an exterior staircase. So, as we approach it, she has tears in her eyes, and I say, "How was your day?"

And she looks at me and she says, "Just devastating." And I say, "Oh, I'm so sorry." And she says, "How bout you?" And I said, "Oh actually, it was actually fine, it was fine. I was—" But I can't really tell her about my time in the military history library and seeing Sam there, you know, kind of contentedly going through his military history book and examining the statues, because she seems so upset.

But she's upset in a kind of romantic way—and I realize that she probably was at one of those arts or literature series of programs. And maybe she's been writing and got very emotional because she's been making—writing poetry or engaging with literature.

I want to ask her what made her feel devastated by the day, but I wonder whether it had something to do with Arta, or with the poem she was writing, but I'm not going to ask her because it seems like it would just make her more upset. So, we're both going to head back towards our dorm.

I have been participating in a secret revolutionary society, and the police are onto us. I am fleeing with Nere and Cat M. down a path between shrubs, in a garden—we are walking quickly, hoping to escape unnoticed. We agree that if captured, we will deny, deny, deny.

I realize that up ahead, more police are waiting— we are trapped.

I understand I will be tortured and maybe killed. I will not turn any of my compatriots in—I am resolved to die if necessary. I cannot help my loved ones and family and friends now. I review my life and am glad I wrote the books.

I've been helping run a large conference for teens and adults with a theme around social justice and genocide. As the conference is concluding, I decide to dart back to the college campus because I would like to obtain a giveaway, to give to every conferee.

I zip across the campus, into a performing arts building, and downstairs to a small unobtrusive door where I know Jeff R. runs his operation. I open the door and begin to try grab several hundred posters for a movie he is screening on campus very soon. This beautiful poster will be a great gift to the conferees, and Jeff will be happy that I'm publicizing his movie event.

The package with all the movie posters has costumes on hangers mixed in with the posters—the costumes are for children—not full-scale theater costumes, more like drugstore Halloween outfits. I don't wish to take these as gifts—only the posters.

Jeff is there, in the office, and he says, "So, what's your thinking on the newspaper?"

I know that he's been waiting to hear if I want to be a volunteer on his campus newspaper project. I don't have time to do this, but now that I'm actually in his office and grabbing several hundred of his posters, I realize that I'm going to agree to help him after all.

I am driving my van, and Ellen is following me, driving a black limousine. We pull into the circular drive of a deluxe hotel and get out of our cars. I tell her we should pull onward into the parking lot, but she says there's no need—the management won't tow these large vehicles or anything, while we're inside.

We go in, and up stairways to the second level. There's a lot of people going from ballroom to ballroom—it's an art exhibition. Very heavily attended. As we're entering a ballroom ourselves, to look at the show, I see, among a crowd of other people, my parents, looking at art on the wall. They look like they did in their last year—my father stooped; my mother equally stooped.

I don't want them to see me. I leave that ballroom and go to another. Ellen trails behind me. Again, I see my parents, inspecting art, in the crowd. I once again avoid their line of sight, pushing through to another part of the room. However, they are now moving towards me. Ellen doesn't understand my erratic movements. I crouch down in front of a couch, to avoid their gaze.

But they have seen me, and they approach. My father has a vacant grin—he is in his dementia period. My mother's face is a mask of concern and worry. A familiar look that I interpret as judging me. Both of their faces are immobile. Ellen is bending over me, urging me to talk with them. I say to them, and to Ellen, "We better go back down and park those cars!" Ellen says, "No, they won't tow us. The cars are too big for that."

I have snapped into a performative mode for the benefit of my parents. I do not want them to witness me and Ellen arguing. I am annoyed that I'm forced to pretend that all is well, but this is what they want me to do, and I know it very well. So, I say, "Okay! Well, then, I guess let's all get dinner!"

Coming from large parking garage, with Sarah (adult-aged), through a door, I have an oversized book wrapped in brown paper. Water has been flooding from an upper garage level, and the water has splashed onto the book's paper cover. I hope the book maybe wasn't damaged?

Through this door we've entered a gigantic clear-span warehouse-like room, well lit, crowded with groups of people. There is a game going on, which Sarah knows how to play. It's very complicated, and there are fluid teams forming and shifting among the many players.

A young man, taller than me, approaches Sarah and me, smiling. He greets us—Sarah is comfortable being approached by a stranger, since this game is going on. He looks at me and says, "Can you guess my name? Tell me yours." I answer, and, he simultaneously says, "Andrew Laties."

I say, "You and I have the same name?" I reach into my pocket and rifle through my wallet, looking for my driver's license, to prove my name. I find it, and he looks at it and sees that it is indeed my name, Andrew Laties. Meanwhile, he has now produced a pre-printed check, and on his check, I can read the name "Andrew Ekdahl."

I side-comment to Sarah, "Ekdahl...it sounds a little like Laties, but it's not the same."

I pull Sarah aside and begin to speculate about the charming young fellow. "He must have done research online about us ahead of time—maybe he wanted to befriend you, to take advantage of you during this game, and thought pulling this little stunt would make you feel relaxed around him. Or maybe he's an FBI handler who has been tasked with manipulating me."

I am aware that Sarah is dubious about my paranoia.

I have crossed the street from the fancy hotel, with Michelle Obama. Over here in the parking lot, on an upper level, we are making love. I'm inside her, when I realize Barack Obama is driving across the street in a gigantic cement mixer. I hear his voice. I pull out of Michelle, before coming. She stands and I marvel at her beautiful body.

Barack calls out, "Are you fucking my wife?"

Michelle seems unrepentant and looks away from him, but I answer, "No!"

I figure that since I didn't actually come inside her, I am not technically lying.

Anyway, he's driving his cement mixer around, while I try grab my pants from the corner of the parking lot. He seems not particularly angry or concerned, more simply energetic and outgoing. Actually, rather sportsmanlike about it all.

I'm glad that Michelle seems perfectly composed. I know she likes me.

Participating in protest rally, in India—lots of people shouting and forming a line confronting the use of elephants for military.

There's a flying baby elephant with tusks fitted out as guns. An explosion blows the flying baby elephant's trunk off, leaving an explosively bleeding gash in the face. This horrific event was livestreamed and immediately gets millions of views.

A new house—my young family is hosting a housewarming party. My kids are running around—the house is modern and very tightly designed—no wasted space.

People have brought housewarming gifts, including animals, for the children. A cage with canaries, a cage with some large insect (beetles?), and a rat. An owl is perched in the corner. Several large fluffy chickens are strutting around.

The children love playing with the animals. They are all in the kitchen, at first, but now I am in the living room and a chicken is walking around there.

Now it flutters up onto my shoulder. I reach up to stroke it—it's very mild and well-groomed. I figure it wants to be fed, but I don't know what it would eat. I'm worried it will poop all over, but it hasn't done that.

It hops down and away among a crowd of guests. I try follow it and see a very long-legged bird which surely cannot be my chicken. I call to it, but then realize it belongs to the next-door-neighbor's child, who looks up at me wondering what I'm doing?

I see my own chicken going back over to my kitchen. I go over there and try block up the exit from the kitchen—there's no door to it, since the floorplan is open, so I am constructing a barrier composed of an ironing board and some planks.

But I tell people, "It's no use! The animals will be everywhere pretty soon."

I'm smiling—I don't really care, the kids don't care, it's fine if the animals have the run of the house.

I am in Melba Tolliver's apartment, or a wardrobe or closet of her apartment. And she has packed up many boxes and suitcases of her clothing and supplies that she needs to bring with her to go on a trip because she's going to be doing a series of on-air appearances—probably to promote her book—and these suitcases and boxes that she's packed up are clothes and make-up and whatever you need to make an on-air appearance.

So, she's packed these up and I'm there to assist her to carry them.

And we wheel these stacks of boxes and suitcases out into the hallway. And there are two elevators next to each other that are open, and we jam the stuff into one elevator. There are already some people in this elevator. She gets in first, and then we put all these boxes and suitcases in. But this elevator is now full and there are still some more boxes and suitcases to go.

So, I bring some of the boxes and suitcases into the second elevator, which is right next to the first elevator. And so, I'm gonna go separately from Melba, using this elevator.

So, I get into my elevator, she's in her elevator, her elevator door closes. I am in my elevator, and to make it close I press a button. The elevator door closes, and the elevator begins to go. The idea is that we're gonna meet up at the bottom.

So, my elevator goes—initially, I have pressed the wrong button apparently because it goes up. But then I press the "1" and then I can feel it going down.

And it goes down for a while, and then it opens, and I take the bags and suitcases out, but Melba's not there. I'm not sure whether her elevator arrived earlier than mine or what. But anyway, I've got all these suitcases and boxes of Melba's.

Well—before, back up at the top, before we had been forced to separate into the two elevators, I had got my airline ticket and my passport, and I was wearing an unfamiliar—somebody else's shirt and coat for some reason. And I had put the ticket and the passport into a pocket as I was talking to the group of people in the elevator—and THEN I had gone to the second elevator.

So now—I've arrived at sort of the ground floor. And I'm in the concourse of an airport—maybe this was an airport hotel that we were in. So, I've gotten separated from Melba, but I do have the ticket and passport in this unfamiliar jacket that I'm wearing, I've got all her bags and suitcases, and now I figure even though I'm separated from her, I'll probably meet up with her—she'll show up at the gate.

So, I'm trying to wheel this large number of boxes and suitcases through this airport concourse—and—we're going to Prague. And I've arrived at the correct airport gate, and it's very crowded, there's really a lot of people going on this airplane.

And I see a whole bunch of my family—my sister Claire's children including their wives are there, but I don't see Melba.

But my nephew Duncan is there. And—so we're waiting at the gate, and I check—I pat my pocket to make sure the passport and the ticket are there, and I definitely feel that there's a lump in my pocket. And finally, the boarding line is boarding, and I get to the front of the line—I've still got all my bags and boxes—evidently, I didn't check them. I guess I'm just going to bring them onto the plane.

And, so there's the ticket-taker, and I reach into my pocket to take out the ticket and the passport, and I find that—as—I was wearing an unfamiliar jacket, somebody else's jacket—and this lump in the pocket, I take it out and it's some garbage, it's not my ticket and my passport, that wasn't what the lump was. It's like a crumpled-up cup and some feathers.

So then—there's a line behind me, and I'm right at the ticket guy, so I say, "Just a second, wait a minute." So, I start patting down and feeling all the pockets in this coat and all the pockets in my shirt and—I can't find the passport and my tickets. And there's people behind me waiting to get on.

So, I take all these boxes and suitcases of Melba's, and I kind of step aside from the line, so people can board ahead of me while I'm frantically searching for these tickets—I'm sure I had it. I remember when I was up on the elevator at first putting them into the pocket. And I go very systematically through each pocket of the jacket and of the shirt and of the pants, and I find things in various of the pockets. Some of the pockets are empty. None of them seem to be the ticket and the passport. And I'm talking with my sister Nancy about how certain I was that I'd put them into my pocket.

And then as I'm going around through these pockets again, I suddenly realize that there is a pocket that I'd never seen on any kind of shirt before. It's on my right chest, sort of high, near my collarbone, there's this zipper pocket. And I can look down on it, and it says, specifically "Passport." And I realize it's a special, unusual passport zipper pocket on the shirt. And I unzip that, and there is the ticket and the passport. And I realize, oh yeah, of course, it's a passport pocket, I've never had one on a shirt before, but that's why I put it into that particular pocket.

So, then I announce, "I found it! I found it!" And—so now I'm able to board the plane—cause I have the passport and the tickets—with all Melba's stuff.

And the next scene, I'm in Prague, and I'm kind of wandering through Prague. And Prague is a pleasant European city, with very nice people.

And I find myself kind of in the outskirts. And it's not Prague anymore—I've arrived at the Smith's house, which is near my childhood home outside of Rochester, New York.

And Mr. Smith is there. Jimmy Smith, who is the boy I knew, who was my friend and then turned into a bully, Jimmy Smith is not there, but the father is there. And he was a schoolbus driver and he's still there. And he is still a schoolbus driver even though it's sixty years later. So, he's pretty old but he looks in good shape. He looks a lot like my ex-father-in-law.

So, I begin to chat with him about, "Oh, you still driving the schoolbus?" And he is still driving the schoolbus.

And I have thought recently about how I could be a schoolbus driver—I would be a good schoolbus driver because I get along with the kids.

And I knew that Mr. Smith was kind of a gruff schoolbus driver, and I say, "So, are the kids—are there a lot of immigrants now among your kids?"

And he gets very irritated, and he says, "Ah, there's too many immigrants, they're ruining the country, there's all these immigrant kids."

And I say, "Well, there's wars going on all over the world, and that's why families have had to leave places like—"

At this point Rebecca has showed up. And Sam is with me too. And Sam has not wanted to go out and play anywhere, he's just hanging around. He's about eight years old. And—he wants a shoulder ride, and I've got him behind me.

And I say to Rebecca and to Mr. Smith, "Well, there's wars in places like Somalia and suppose that you're a middle-class office-worker, and you've got a nice house, in a city in Somalia, and suddenly there's a war, and bombs dropping by your house—and you know, you gotta leave, you know you gotta leave. And—Iraq, there's all these middle-class people, suppose you're just an office-worker and your family's living in a nice house, just like this one, and suddenly there's shooting and there's bombing, and you've gotta pick up your kids and you leave. So that's why there's all these refugees and immigrants. And they come to places like this, the suburbs here, and then—it used to be that they were at home, but now they're a refugee. And it's a child and so that's why your schoolbus has got a lot of refugees and immigrants on it. It's not that they're bad people, it's that they had a terrible situation—they had to run away from a war. Or get killed."

And Mr. Smith seems slightly mollified that maybe it's not the children's fault that they have to be crowding onto his bus.

And he says to Sam, "You know, you could go into the house–you know Jimmy's not around, but you could play in his room if you want to look around."

And I say, "Yeah, Sam, you could just go up and look around in Jimmy's room if you want, he's probably got some stuff to see."

But Sam has no interest in going into the house and looking at Jimmy Smith's old room. He just—he's kind of shy and wants to hang around me.

I see a video on my phone in which a woman is caressing a mule's head—it's her pet mule, he's gray-colored and very adorable. The woman tells how her mule is such a perfect pet. I think, hey, I should get a mule for a pet too!

On a pad of notebook paper, I write, in pen, the words "Mule as a pet." I then tap the words with my finger. I seem to think that the paper will go to a webpage and get me an answer. The paper doesn't do it, and I tap the paper more sharply. I thought this was some new kind of paper that accesses the Internet! Finally, it works, and a selection of YouTube videos appears on the paper. I click on one.

A video starts playing in which a mule is in a yard eating grass and weeds. The voice-over says that mules are great because they can keep your yard in good shape.

I write on the page "Cost of a mule," and when I tap it, a page comes up with a tally of expenses that show it costs $9,258 to obtain a mule, and they come shipped directly from Australia, in a crate. I feel a surge of despair that it would be so expensive, but it doesn't surprise me too much. Of course, everything you want is expensive. I'm surprised the mule could survive a trip from Australia in a crate, but I suppose it must be normal.

However—I am thinking that I should make more of an effort to learn of any possible downsides to the mule. I click on a different YouTube video. This time it's a man, and he's walking around his farm and saying that a mule can eat pretty much anything. If your trees have excess fruit, like oranges—and here there's film of a mule eating oranges off a tree—well, the mule will take care of your excess. In fact, the mule also loves to eat wild berries.

I am realizing that since I don't have fruit trees or berry bushes, it might be an issue for me to satisfy a hungry mule.

Now the man is inside a church, and he says, the mule also will gnaw on pretty much anything, so, you do need to be careful about that. The film shows the mule wandering among the pews in the church, eating the cushions, and biting the seats. The man says, look! He's even eating these gargoyles! And, indeed now the mule is seen biting statues and gargoyles in the church.

By this point I have realized that I really would not have the time or skill to oversee a mule.

Driving down country road and among fields in valley towards rustic restaurant—elegantly built out of former barn. There's an outdoor bar, with pleasant outdoor seating at round tables. Dozens of diners, the bar is busy. This restaurant is next door to my house, which is also a large, reconstructed barn that has become this unusual country-style house.

We've arrived at the restaurant and as we're waiting to be seated, I see that it is on fire. Flames are licking up from behind the bartenders, and from various places at the edges. The diners and waiters are ignoring this fire, or, maybe not aware of it. The fire doesn't appear to be spreading—it's like a feature of the restaurant—but I do feel concern that if it suddenly grows and becomes larger it could jump from the restaurant next door, over to my house, and set my house on fire.

I understand that the restaurant management may be choosing to ignore their fire because dousing it with lots of water would ruin the décor and the fixtures and equipment and ruin the business. Similarly, a targeted use of flame-retardant fire-extinguishers would damage the restaurant. And look at all the business they're doing! So—they can't interrupt things to put out the fire. And really, the fire has not yet exploded into a firestorm—but it could do so at any time. I'm seated at the table, quite concerned, but not talking with the waiter about it.

A road through a cut in a hill—dirt road, rather steep, which I've driven up and back on regularly. Each time I go back and forth, there are more raggedy people sitting by the side of the road— homeless people. It seems that they are being directed to gather there or move to there. Bleachers have been set up on either side of the road to accommodate them.

I'm setting up a large white sheet, vertically, against the road-side wall—I will draw or paint on this. But I realize there's a sort of panel inset into the wall, behind my sheet. I pry the panel loose and there's a tall man who seems dead in standing position right behind there. He immediately starts falling forward, and I quickly jam the panel back into place. I suspect he is alive, but unconscious.

Invisible wizard whipping invisible knight riding invisible white tiger.

Tiger becomes visible and makes subservient crouch, urging wizard to mount its back.

In doctor's office, had to sit on stake up my rectum— medical diagnostic procedure. Unpleasant and irritating.

Then—I had five extra tiny penises that had sprouted off my regular penis. Was told, in medical office, to put on a covering like a diaper. Went into another office and lay down on white gurney. I don't know what the doctor is going to do. I wonder, would the extra penises work—might be nice to have extra sex? Or is the doctor going to circumcise them, or amputate them so that the blood flow is better to the main one? He was in the room briefly, but he left.

Now he returns—he's got dressed in a green suit with a tie. He puts a big video screen onto my belly, and there's a big screen on the wall behind him. He begins a full-scale sales pitch to me about how Charles Lloyd is an esteemed, old saxophone player and now his children Susan and John are raising money for his eldercare.

When I realize that the doctor is doing a fundraising pitch while I'm pinned down in this embarrassing situation, I sit up, push the video screen off, and say, "You think you can just demand I participate in your fundraising scheme right now? This is inappropriate! Fuck you!" I storm out of the office, even though I'm barely covered.

WHICH WAY UP IS THIS?

I arrive at cash desk in the morning (Eric Carle Museum Bookstore desk) and see a post-it note-envelope labeled "Sucker Gift." I unfold the note, and it says, "You have a present!"

Then I notice a paper bag to the side of the cash desk, which is quivering. I go around to the inside of the cash desk and see that in the bag is a puppy. A brown terrier, very small, standing with its tongue out. Incredibly cute, sort of trembling.

I reach into the bag and take the puppy into my arms. It is so affectionate, cuddling and licking. I feel overwhelmed with love for the puppy, but I realize that because I'm allergic to dogs, I cannot keep it. Plus—I don't have time to care for a puppy!

I have a toddler, and a baby, with me, plus some employees are around. The baby seems entranced by the puppy, but the toddler appears to be jealous. Anyway, I say, "This is a wonderful surprise—but—I am allergic."

One of my staff says, "Look, though, here are your allergy packs." And I see that included with the puppy are two devices. They are mechanical air-filtering machines—one is for the store, and one is for my house. So, I would set these up and it would make it possible for me to have the puppy even though I'm allergic.

I'm confused. The feelings of love for the puppy, mixed with my sense of obligation to this dog, go along with a wish not to take all the responsibility. For instance—doesn't the dog need to be walked immediately? Has he been sitting in the bookstore for hours in the bag?

Now I am outside, walking up a steep street— going to a store to buy supplies to care for the puppy, and I am approached by a tall woman who slightly resembles Michelle Obama. The woman says, "Did I hear that you have a new pet?"

I realize that this grinning woman was one of a group of my customers who were secretly behind me receiving the gift puppy. Now I know that I can't possibly refuse the puppy.

Renee is my landlord for an apartment. She mentions that the tenant before me, coincidentally, was also a shakuhachi player.

I will now be moving out of the apartment, and I say to Renee, "You should try rent to a shakuhachi player again—it seems like it's that kind of apartment. In fact, it seems like a signal that you and Keith should go to Japan! You are a timpani player so you should study taiko!"

Renee and Keith give me a pained look, and I realize that her battle with cancer makes them feel like they really will never go to Japan—although they are Buddhists and surely would like to. I realize that there's another way for them to go there. I say, "Well, you don't have to travel there—you can be reincarnated there!"

Saying this makes me remember the old Hindu adage that it's better to be born an ant, in India, then to be born a human being anywhere else in the world. I wonder if it's the same with Japan. To be born in Japan means you're closer to enlightenment, in terms of sequence of rebirths. I think—gosh—maybe I will be reborn in Japan myself?

I am in my bookstore. It's busy. Spike Lee, Patti Smith, and a young artist who reminds me of Yoko Ono are all walking through the store, towards the exit. I stop them, and remark that I just was having a dream in which we were right here. In my dream—I inform them—I was telling them about my newest book.

The Yoko-Ono-like woman is smiling, and she says she would very much like to read it. I say, oh—you want to read it? Just a moment, I will grab a copy. I dart back, past the cash register, to where I should have a few copies of my newest book. It is a slim volume with an eggshell-blue colored jacket. However, to my perplexity, there are piles of empty yellow photo-film boxes on the floor—it's kind of messy there by the register—and my copies of my new book aren't there. I scan again—definitely no copies.

I think—well—maybe she would read another of my books—the Ursonate book? I see however that there are none of my other books on that shelf beyond the register either.

I think, well, maybe because we had just moved bookstores, and everything is rearranged, I need to check over by the poetry section.

I know that Spike Lee, Patti Smith, and the Yoko-Ono-woman wish to leave—I don't want to hold them up. I rapidly go to the poetry shelves of the bookstore—but here too—I don't see any of my recent books. I think—maybe she would like to read *Rebel Bookseller*? But I don't see any copies of that either.

I return to the three of them. I apologize and say, well—I'm so sorry I can't find a copy just now. Anyway, for next time, I'll be sure to set aside a copy for you when I get some more copies.

I'm especially baffled, as they leave—because my new book—the blue-colored one—is my best book. I am trying to remember what it's about—what's in it. I simply can't remember what exactly this book is—I only know that it was my best.

I'm entering Phillipsburg on Route 22, around the bend, in a vehicle—a car maybe—it's night-time and the road and city are almost entirely dark, without streetlights or houselights. There are a few gas stations and fast-food places along the road in the distance but otherwise the roadway is very dark. I had spoken in the past with Phen about his failure to convince the city to illuminate this roadway with streetlights, or to require that some lighting be in place.

As we drive along, I hold up my iPhone and turn on its flashlight—it casts a sharp light outwards and to my surprise reveals a party scene—apparently a wedding reception in a field by the side of the road.

I am no longer driving in the car but am floating about this nighttime scene of women in dresses at tables, during a wedding reception. But some of the women, in elaborate white dresses, are passed out drunk, lying on the grass. My spotlight illuminates their prone forms as these appear out of the darkness and then vanish as I pan my light.

Now I have continued to drive in to the city, to the airport. In the airport departure lounge, it is very crowded and I'm at a store buying food to bring onto the plane. I think I should eat a lot right now— although it's ten in the morning—because I won't have a chance to eat dinner until after the plane lands

WHICH WAY UP IS THIS?

tonight at six pm. So, I am buying and immediately eating a chicken sandwich. But as I return to the gate, to wait in line with Rebecca to get onto the plane, she questions why I haven't brought much food with me.

I tell her that I had a conversation about this already with Tagor. We both agree that we don't need to bring a lot of food onto the plane. It's better to eat here in the airport. Rebecca should eat here. I offer her some food.

Now we are on the plane, and they are bringing us dinner. It turned out there was no problem after all—they were always going to be feeding us on the plane, all along and we needn't have worried.

Searching my bookstore for book by Emberley or Zelensky about round-the-world theme. Customer is large woman with small child. I had sold lots of copies, in paperback picture book edition, but now seem to be out of stock. I tell her I will reorder.

January 1, 2025. I'm reading a social media blogpost by Ann K., who narrates this recursive tale:

The other day, Ann was listening to NPR radio and was surprised to be hearing an interview with someone she had once met: Jessica S., owner of Greenlight Bookstore. During this radio interview, Jessica was recommending a book—a graphic novel.

Ann already knew that Jessica liked that graphic novel, and Ann started listening to the radio interview more carefully.

To Ann's surprise, Jessica continued her recommendation by beginning to tell a tale of being engaged in first reading this book while on a train ride, and of how a woman riding beside her on that train had taken an interest in this book Jessica was reading. Jessica said this train seatmate had introduced herself as Ann K.

Ann, now hearing this radio broadcast, was of course riveted and taken aback—and wondering how much of this accidental interaction—which had taken place months prior—would be revealed to the world.

Jessica continued, and told how, she had of course been happy to tell her seatmate Ann about the book: it was a graphic novel written by a Japanese author, recently translated and released into the US market. The story was a first-person narrative from the perspective of a young teenage girl whose older brother had died.

Ann—listening to the radio—realized that Jessica intended to tell the entire story of their meeting. She felt embarrassed, but did trust Jessica.

Jessica continued: on hearing this plot point, Ann had revealed that her own older brother had died when Ann was a young teen.

Jessica continued her tale, saying of course she had expressed sorrow to hear this—and then confided that she too, as a teen, had suffered the death of her older brother. The two strangers, on learning suddenly of their shared grief, had embraced and begun crying.

Now listening to this radio broadcast Ann once again began to cry.

Jessica continued. She and Ann had realized together that it was the book—the graphic novel—that had awakened their profound shared emotion. Ann told how she had been a drama teacher and school headmistress for decades, sharing her love of books with young women; it was amazing how books could change lives. Jessica explained she was a bookseller and bookstore owner and agreed the experience they'd just had showed the power of books to create connection.

I became half-awake and recalled the story I'd read aloud to Rebecca last night about the woman in Japan who'd experienced enlightenment, after the death of her beloved son, through Zen practice with the "Mu" koan—an enlightenment experience that reunited her with her son, through her awakened awareness of nonduality.

I thought about the proverb "If you meet the Buddha on the road, kill him." I realized—in light of the Zen woman's awakening statement, "I am the Buddha"—that I, and the Buddha, and the road, are one. It is impossible to meet the Buddha on the road, since I am the Buddha, and I am the road, and if I meet the Buddha on the road, then I must kill this delusive-version-of-Buddha, that is, destroy my delusion of separation.

I realized this is what happened when Ann and Jessica experienced simultaneously the awareness that they shared identical grief. The moment of their empathetic embrace and tears was the collapse of separation.

The recursive moment of Ann hearing Jessica on the radio was again duality's collapse.

ANDREW LATIES co-founded Easton Book Festival, Book & Puppet Company, Vox Pop, The Children's Bookstore, Children's Bookfair Company, Chicago Children's Museum Store, Eric Carle Museum Bookstore, and PovertyFighters.com. He managed Bank Street Bookstore. He shared the 1987 Women's National Book Association's Pannell Award for bringing children and books together. His *Rebel Bookseller: Why Indie Businesses Represent Everything You Want to Fight For—From Free Speech to Buying Local to Building Communities* won the 2006 Independent Publisher Award and is available in a second edition from Seven Stories Press.

ALSO BY ANDREW LATIES

NONFICTION

Living Ur Sonata

The Music Thief

Rebel Bookseller: Why Indie Businesses Represent Everything You Want to Fight For—From Free Speech to Buying Local to Building Communities

Son of Rebel Bookseller: A Very Large Homework Assignment

MUSIC

Three Fates Sing Ur Sonata (with Urchestra)

Thou Art Continuous (With Eric Blitz)

And then I ended up having a conversation with someone about these Ardmore and Hazel editorial projects, and the revelations that were made of their— these editors that had sort of created these bowdlerized versions of the originals, and then the additional rounds of editorial work which was digging up the real—the originals and the original meanings.

So, I had befriended several of Veronica's managers, including a middle-aged guy and a sort of hipster guy, and I was being invited to—I guess I was there a second day also—and I was invited to start ringing on the register.

And I asked, "Oh, you want me to work the register?" And the guy was like, "Yeah, so you can participate." And I was like, "Oh, so, you just gonna throw me in there?" And he said, "Sure, just do it." And I said, "Ok, well, what system—what computer system are you using?" And he looked at me and he said, "Oh, we don't have that." And I realized that they didn't have a computerized inventory, and they did everything by hand, on like pieces of paper.

And I said, "Wow, this is really—this is what they call a poor people's bookstore isn't it? You just grew from being this little used bookstore—just doing nothing, and you sort of skipped steps along the way, that's like a case study. You know, you could be packaging this up into a sort of corporate presentation, and Veronica could be on the road, and charging ten thousand dollars for half a day giving corporate presentations on how you created this place. But she would never want to do that."

And he said, "Well, I don't know, that sounds terrible. And would you want to do that?"

And I said, "Well I should be doing that." And I actually planned to do it for More Than Words—which was across the street and was a nonprofit that had a different vibe—it was a more glossy nonprofit—where I was supposed to go later in the day.

And then at sometime early on the second day, I called Veronica—I was with her on the phone—and I started gushing complimentary things, I said, "It's amazing! You did this! You were the person who really made this happen."

And as I was saying this to her, she went completely silent, and I realized that I was on the verge of telling her that I was in love with her, but I stopped myself because I knew that, that wouldn't be helpful. It wouldn't be helpful to her or me. So, I didn't.

And then, I was talking with her about her plan for later in the day and when the author should start reading, who was going to be coming, and I said, "Wow, you know what happened yesterday was, you know, you thought no-one was going to come, and then more and more people came, and finally a huge number of people had come and, luckily you took that space where you could accommodate them, that was amazing you had the foresight to recognize that people were really going to come out."